THE SMOKING BOOK

THE
SMOKING BOOK

Lesley Stern

THE UNIVERSITY OF CHICAGO PRESS   CHICAGO AND LONDON

LESLEY STERN was born in Zimbabwe and lives in Sydney, Australia, where she teaches film and theatre at the University of New South Wales. She is the author of *The Scorsese Connection* (1995).

The University of Chicago Press, Chicago 60637
The University of Chicago Press, Ltd., London
© 1999 by The University of Chicago
All rights reserved. Published 1999
Printed in the United States of America

08 07 06 05 04 03 02 01 00 99   1 2 3 4 5

Library of Congress Cataloging-in-Publication Data

Stern, Lesley
    The smoking book / by Lesley Stern.
         p. cm.
    ISBN 0-226-77330-2 (alk. paper)
    1. Cigarette smokers Fiction. 2. Smoking—Psychological aspects
Fiction. 3. Smoking—Social aspects Fiction. 4. Tobacco habit
Fiction. 5. Smoking.   I. Title.
PR9619.3.S796S64   1999
823—dc21   99-26219
                                         CIP

∞

For the friends I grew up with in Zimbabwe,
still friends today—Annette E., Jane N., Lesley R., Gillian W.

CONTENTS

ACKNOWLEDGMENTS

I am grateful to the Getty Research Institute for inviting me to be a visiting scholar for the year of 1998, thus making it possible for me to complete the book; and to the Department of English, University of Queensland, for offering me the Brooks Visiting Fellowship, which provided the opportunity of a month's concentrated writing in 1996. I thank the staff of the National Archives of Zimbabwe for their help.

Versions of various parts of this book have been published in *No substitute: prose, poems, images*, ed. T. White, A. Gibbs, W. Jenkins, and N. King (Perth: Fremantle Arts Centre Press, 1990); *Southerly* 52, no.1 (March 1992); *Heat*, no.2 (1996); *Trafic* (March 1999); and *Critical Inquiry* 25 (spring 1999).

SMOKE CIRCLES

Before waking in the morning there is a memory, or anticipation—coffee fumes, tendrils of thick blue smoke, French
tobacco, you.

Last moments of the night, I breathe smoke into your
mouth, watch you absorb this gift so thoughtlessly, so greedily. Your sleepy sensuous appetite wakes again, for a moment,
a wanting-more in me. Then you slowly exhale, smoke circles, touches our skin, puts desire to sleep.

BURNOUT

∞

At first she is entranced by his speech: his words play over her body, she trembles, she sleeps to his murmurous allusions, awakens to his ardent admonitions.

Time passes. She loses a word here and there, drifts in and out of his consciousness, finds herself on the edge of sanity; if she were to slip, she would spiral down down into the big black hole, consigned forever to silence and ineluctable night. She does not know whether this is death or a reprieve. As she sways on the verge of the precipice, he woos her again—she remembers the serenity, the rapture of narcosis. How can she resist?

Drifting, she is drawn into another place, a far country where there are no words; on the borders of this country they lie abandoned, tarnished, like angels fallen from flight. The odd vagrant word somehow penetrates, permeates the atmosphere, but it cannot last and soon will evaporate. Sometimes she hears his voice, in the distance, obscure, calling her name: "Aramarena, Aramarena." She listens to the cadence falling, and she thinks: you think because you call me by this name— Aramarena—you think this is my name. You do not know that I have no name, no home, no point of departure, no destination. She whom you call Aramarena is merely a wanderer in a land where the hunchbacked rhinoceros rampages, where dragons devour indiscriminately in pastures of verdant predication, where profligate desire escapes unsentenced.

Returning to him less and less frequently, she finds herself in dispute; where once she was immersed in his speech, now it is hard to lay hands on his words. He has grown wily, begins to employ tricks of the trade, even though he'd never call himself a merchant, far less a middleman. With solicitous foresight he shepherds his words into a discursive field. He constructs boundaries around them, draws what he calls a tentative and tactical circumscription. To her it looks like a speech bubble. He looks more and more like a comic book hero.

"Never underestimate the Phantom!" Her mother's warning returns to her from long ago.

She knows the time has come, a time of reckoning.

She takes the cigarette she is smoking—languidly she holds it between her fingers, her wrist relaxed, suggestive. Slowly she exhales, a smoke ring floats in the air. Then she positions the red glowing tip of her cigarette in the middle of his speech bubble. Around the tip, a brown burn mark spreads, a hole opens up, grows out from the center, consuming all his nestled words. Then, in the bubble, there is just a pile of ash.

She finishes her cigarette, inhaling deeply. It is the last one. She will never smoke again.

SUSPENDED FOREVER

∞

Soft pack, white with a red star emblazoned on the front. You could hold it in the palm of your hand—even a child could close her hand around the pack, hear the cellophane rustle, smell the tobacco: strong, raw, a smell of heat as poles with cured leaves are pulled out from the furnaces.

Star cigarettes: cheap, enduring.

They'd wait till the heat of the day, the dead time, when work stopped on the farm and the adults slept or argued, and they'd steal to the store. For months they've been saving and planning, they know exactly what is needed, precise quantities, precise prices. Still, they linger in the store, after so much calculation their shopping is sensationally inefficient. This is what they enjoy, what they are really here for: the sensations, the indolence. The counter is high—they would have to stand on an old petrol tin to see over—and the storekeeper is cranky about dragging the tin around the front. He needs it to stand on himself, to reach up to the painted tin plates and the row of tinned bully beef. Why should he drag the tin around for kids? If they really want to, they can climb under the counter and he can always tell if roaming fingers start to stick—his head's a seething nest of eyes. If the white boss were here, the storekeeper might call him bwana and he might even move the petrol tin for the kids, but not a chance when they're here by themselves and up to no good. Their no-goodness is no-skin-off-my-nose, which suits everyone all around, allows a pact of sorts between this black man and these small white girls. They don't mind that they can't see over the counter, for this place is like Bluebeard's castle: mysterious, filled with treasures, but out of bounds. If they cross the boundary, if they see with their own eyes the wondrous treasury, then the seething nest will spring to life and they'll be stung, stung right in the eye. They often taunt each other with this threat, cringe and clutch each other, shielding their eyes, for a moment petrified. "Imagine!" they tell each other. "Imagine an arrow in the eye." Then they stagger around drunkenly, mimicking blindness, hooting and wailing, hysterically happy.

Now it's the dead part of the day, dust hangs in the air, infiltrates the lungs, enervates. Inside the store the world comes alive: there's a crackle of subterranean gossip, a clatter of beans ricocheting against tin, volcanic murmur of the sewing machine treadling erratically. Walking in out of the glare, it's as though the cavernous gloom, the density of the beaten earthenware floor, absorbs the jagged edges of daylight living. And as you stand in the cool dimness, you close your eyes and smell: cotton, the pungency of cheap starched cotton, bales of primary colors heaped up behind the tailor, ripped into, shreds littering the ground around his machine. In the gloom, tendrils of blue tobacco smoke unfurl, float through the air, entwining somnolent words. Old mealie sacks are recycled, used for wrapping, still smelling of mealie meal, a textured smell woven into the scene. Pink carbolic soap, sharply acidic, pierces the nostrils.

They crouch on the floor counting their sweaty coins into two piles. One pile is for here; the other is for buying biltong in the butcher's shop next door. Her sister says, "Bags I stay here, you get the biltong." At the very thought of the butcher's shop, nausea sweeps through her body, a stench of raw meat permeates the air, she goes limp at the wrists, her body rendered a bag of sawdust. She sees herself a rag doll split open, spilt out on the floor there to absorb blood dripping from carcasses suspended in the air. "Weed," says the elder sister, but she scoops up one of the piles of coins and backs out into the glare, heading for next door. The younger sister reaches up on tiptoe and nudges her coins across the counter. As the man begins to count out the money, as he turns the transaction into a sardonic ritual, just as he always does, she has a vision of four-and-twenty blackbirds and the queen in a baby blue English hat sitting up in bed eating bread-and-honey sandwiches. The man makes several trips, slowly, as though crossing continents to claim this hidden treasure: two bottles of lukewarm Fanta, three tins of condensed milk, and a pack of Star cigarettes. All the while he ignores her, continues a wordy ramble with the tailor, breaking off now and then to pick up on an altercation about prices with a group of women squatting in the coolest corner, or digressing to shout at the mangy dogs lurking in the doorway— "Humba! Humba!" Everyone in the store takes up the chant —"Humba! Humba!"—there's a flurry and shooing of hands, a scuffling of dogs.

As she carefully packs her purchases into an old and rumpled brown paper bag, she leaves space for the sticks of biltong. She thinks of her sister next door. She sees herself there, sees herself crumpling in a heap, sees the slaughter yards, sees big brown eyes, the gun between, an explosion, herself on the floor of the butcher's shop, covered in sawdust and blood. Adult voices over her head speak of sunstroke, remonstrate about hats.

They don't know. Only her sister understands.

Her hand closes around the pack of Stars. She pulls it out of the brown paper bag and looks intently at the pack, willing this image to erase all sight and sensation of the butcher's shop. It isn't any old star: it's red and shiny and marvelously synthetic, composed of a myriad of tiny sparkling rhinestones. There's a blue lasso caught in midair, emblazoned on the pack. It hovers, suspended forever over the star. You could cut out the star and stick it on cardboard and put a pin through it, and you'd have a sheriff's badge. But there's no way you could nail down that twirling lasso. A smoke ring circling.

At home they add some items to the brown paper bag: a penknife nicked from their father's toolbox—they call it the

Davy Crockett knife; a box of matches; the new *Beano* comic that's just arrived in the mail, rolled up and plastered over with a plethora of pastel stamps. They come irregularly, these parcels, from a faraway place called Scotland, from cousins they've never met but whom they imagine; they imagine them eating lettuce sandwiches and drinking ginger beer and having adventures in underground caves where sparkling streams flow, with sheepdogs who've got names like Timmy.

They hide their stash in an outhouse, biding their time. Soon, they know, their father will disappear for a day, off to a cattle sale from which he will return rollicking and full of tales; and as soon as he's gone, their mother will put on her new dress and get out the jalopy and tell them she's taking some eggs to a neighbor ten miles away. They are on standby, alert, waiting for their moment.

They have wrapped their treasures in a cloth. They used to practice walking with a bundle on their heads, trying to imitate the languorous strolling of the African women, who'd carry great clusters of wood, pitchers of water, who'd laugh and execute little dance steps. When their mother found them practicing, she explained the concept of deportment and told them how Princess Anne had to sit still and silent for a full half hour balancing a book on her head. They gave up practicing. Last Christmas they'd been on a big expedition to town to see a pantomime. They were enthralled by all the dressing up and inspired by Dick Whittington's demeanor. It struck them both as the perfect posture for adventure. So when their moment comes, after their parents have left, they stick a broomstick through their bundle, and taking it in turns hoist it over a shoulder and head off through long brown grass toward the *vlei*.

It seems as though they walk for hours, through the heat, ducking to keep below the grass, dodging flies, rubbing spit into the scratches that appear on their arms and legs. They begin to feel faint. They've eaten only the barest of bones all day, savoring, anticipating. At last they reach the river. A dank brown trickle of water snakes sluggishly through granite rocks worn smooth by ancient torrents. There is no evidence of life now, just an occasional rustle in the grass, in the trees. But there are traces, hoof marks of *mombies* are encrusted in the dried mud. The scene appears immutable; you can't imagine that the rains will come again, that there'll be a yielding underfoot, a churning, a realigning of the landscape. Greenness. Now dust overlays everything, it coats the water and lies heavy on the spindly foliage of the thorn trees. They've been told of other places, like the country their grandparents call Home, where there are picket fences instead of barbed wire, where bluebells grow in woods and children frolic in meadows. They often play a game with the word *meadow*, they toss it in the air, listen to it trilling—it strikes them as a most exotic word, verdant and inviting. They have a chant, an incantation for the summer storms:

> *Rain, rain, go away*
> *come back another day*
> *so Molly and Polly can play*
> *in the meadows.*

Now they tread gingerly over the rocks, taking care not to slip into the bilharzia-infested water. They clamber up a *kopje*, over the rocks to a ledge that is overhung by a cluster of *msasa* trees—magical trees that mix the color of their leaves as randomly as rain falls. Here in the shade they can see down to the dam, they can keep an eye on all tracks through the grass, but the secret is this: they remain invisible. It is a perfect place for feasting. They break off a few young branches and sweep away the droppings that have grown dry and hard and shrunken, sorting them, as they sweep, into piles: Heffalumps from Heaven, Hunyani Hippopotami and the singular Limpopo Leopard. These piles they place in a triangle on the periphery of their terrain to ward off evil and covetous spirits. Then they spread their treasures in a circle on the granite surface—Fanta, condensed milk, biltong, *Beano*, Davy Crockett knife, a flat stone they've found to use as a hammer, and Star cigarettes. Sitting back to back in the middle of this circle, knees scrunched up to their chins, eyes screwed shut, they count backward as fast as possible, racing each other, from a hundred to seventy-three. Then they whip around lunging for the penknife. The elder sister grabs it first, so she gets to rip the tops off the Fantas, but this means that the younger sister gets to perform the shakedown. One bottle in each hand, she jumps up and down yodeling, bloodthirsty. Then they let rip. Hot orange liquid, vivid against the granite backdrop, spurts into the air, drenching the girls; wetness turning sticky in the instant it touches skin, mingling with salt and sweat. They lick themselves, each other, and drink deeply. After the dryness, the heat, their long trek through pirate-infested deserts—what sweet sweet satisfaction.

Now, while one of them holds a can of condensed milk steady, the other positions the blade of the knife over the top of the tin. Clutching the stone in her fist, she hammers till the blade pierces through the container and sticky liquid, creamy colored, trickles out. They turn the tin around and make another hole on the other side. Now, all is ready. They each have a bottle of Fanta and a stick of biltong. They look like beaten leather, these strips of dried meat, so their mother says, but they imagine a much more esoteric derivation: giraffe turds, sinewy and etiolated. They share this first tin of condensed milk just as they will share the other two tins. While one throws her head back and sucks at the tin, the other sucks at her biltong stick, softening the texture, preparing to sink teeth in and tear. There's a wonderful peppery taste, a sensation of smokiness. Shreds of meat lodge in crevices around the mouth so that the flavor of condensed milk is suffused by spiciness.

As they suck and tear and chew, they leaf their way through *Beano*, treating it as a comic play, as though they are animated puppets. While one of them adopts a funny voice and reads out the speech bubbles, the other registers the speech in her body, miming the action. Many years later, after the older sister has died, choked herself on speech, the younger will discover, and lose herself, in a reminiscent theater. A village hall high in the mountains of Japan near Kanazawa, snow and only snow as far as you can see. Except: in the distance a tree bare of foliage, bearing a single cluster of orange persimmons. In the hall it's hot with bodies. She will watch the puppets, hear the farmers narrating in a language familiar yet strangely, exuberantly, comic. Immersed in this performance of primitive Bunraku she will remember, and grieve.

A little later, they are sent to boarding school in a town far away and are wrenched apart. In different dormitories, different classrooms, they think about the *Beano* comics. Here feasts take place at midnight. She is amazed to find that here the practice is to use a tin opener to take the top off the can of condensed milk. Then a spoon is used to scoop out the thick milk. She finds this practice barbaric—it's like shoveling wet cement from one hole to another. In the dormitory in the town she closes her eyes and remembers the scratchiness, the warmth of the granite rock, the tremulous undulating pleasure of sucking. She feels her lips, mouth, the sweet thick creaminess slithering down her throat, burning her chest.

Now, drinking scotch unadulterated, without ice or water, she recaptures that sensation. Though she wonders: is it the primacy of that original landscape where adults were rendered redundant, is this what she recalls? Or is it a more mediated memory, traced already by loss, already adulterated—a midnight memory in a boarding school?

In the bush when they've exhausted the food and drink, when they're satisfied, or almost, they turn over and lie on their stomachs side by side, propped on their elbows. The litany begins:

Let's tell a story.
What will the story be about?

Snakes?

    or

Fires?

    or

Murders?

They toss a bottle top to decide who'll start. Then, before the story begins, they tear the cellophane on the pack of Stars, ease two cigarettes out, roll them around between their fingers, place them between their lips, and light up.

When their father comes into the house from the fields, he pours a large cup of cold tea and slurps it, stuffs his mouth with huge chunks of Christmas cake that've been sitting on the tray waiting for him all morning even though it isn't Christmas. Then he leans back, lights up a cigarette, and inhales deeply. They all breathe deeply, reassured, now they can speak. He twirls the used match in his fingers and suddenly, deftly, he sends it spinning—like a javelin it soars, disappears into thin air. Someone else will pick it up.

The first deep breath they take, drawing in the nicotine, is sickening; nausea wells up and their bodies are shaken by coughing. As the spasms subside they stub out, but do not relinquish, the cigarettes. They agree to pretend.

The story begins. The narrator uses her cigarette as a wand: to gesticulate, to make a point, to hold the world in suspension. It is a wand that commands attention, spellbinds an audience, dramatizes, entrances.

Then and now: there's a blue lasso caught in midair. It hovers, suspended forever over a star, red and shiny and marvelously synthetic.

A FISHY SMELL

∞

But let a noise or a scent, once heard or once smelt, be heard or smelt again in the present and at the same time in the past, real without being actual, ideal without being abstract. . . . A minute freed from the order of time . . . one can understand that the word "death" should have no meaning for him; situated outside time, why should he fear the future?   MARCEL PROUST, *Remembrance of Things Past*

On the No. 73 bus, in a grim London winter, you contemplate there being no future. The man next to you takes a small packet, glistening golden green, out of the enormous pocket of his gray overcoat. Ceremoniously he opens it up and starts shaking strands of tobacco into the palm of his hand, teases out the filaments, rolling and kneading, and as he does so the tobacco exudes a sharp distinctive pungency. The bus is filled with a warm aroma. All at once you feel the heat rising in the tobacco barn in Africa, the golden color of the leaves as they are pulled out from the ovens and the overwhelming smell that seems to seep through the floor and the walls, through the sound of Shona voices and into your body. A minute freed from the order of time.

The odor of addiction, the persistence of memory. These tobacco emanations constitute a kind of olfactory history, and science tells its story. It goes like this: molecules from an odor source reach the receptor cells of the olfactory epithelium (that is, the nostrils). The cells produce electrical impulses for transmission by nerve fibers to the olfactory bulb of the brain. Some signals go on to the limbic system, which is involved in memory and emotion. This is the thing about the body and its sensations: they're real, though they may well be real without being actual, ideal without being abstract. The body isn't a simple information system—signals seldom travel through it in capsules as though through space, they seldom arrive at a single destination, uncontaminated.

This smell of tobacco, summoning childhood sensations from the past, suffuses the present with a sense of plenitude; but it also involves anticipation, opens up a hunger, a pit in the stomach that craves feeding. It acts like the smell of food: bacon and eggs when you're hungover and dehydrated; tangy smoked fish in an open-air market; spices roasting in the oven; mealies cooked over coals; the juicy smell released when you crush garlic; the odor that envelopes you as you walk beneath a mango tree heavy with fruit, overripe, about to fall squishily to the ground. Tobacco smells in the way that food smells, but it differs from food in that it is consumed neither in its natural state nor cooked; rather, it is incinerated so the smoke thus released can be inhaled. For these reasons Lévi-Strauss assigns tobacco a metaculinary or intermediary status since it is neither raw nor cooked. Or we could say it is both. The pivotal role that has fallen to tobacco in various symbolic systems ("tobacco symbolizes the symbolic," says Derrida) comes from the fact that it unites contradictory values. It functions in discursive economies that bring together opposites but leave a gap between them—like synapses, where a jump has to be made, and in the jumping the message might swerve in midair, be deflected.

Meanings somersault.

This gnawing hunger that is provoked by the smell of tobacco, by a memory of plenitude, demands that something be taken into the body, that wanting be transformed into satisfaction. But tobacco smoke is not ingested like food, which is absorbed, and after absorption the remainder ejected as piss or vomit or crap. Smoking involves an ingestion of which nothing remains and thus might appear as pure expenditure, satisfaction without loss, pleasure without labor. Yet, of course, smoke circulates in both a psychic economy (which involves the exploitation of desire) and a political economy (which involves the exploitation of labor, traditionally cheap labor in the colonies). After labor is converted, there is indeed a remainder of sorts, but it glistens, and instead of crap it's called surplus value.

There is an old photograph I often reach for, as a reminder of the remainder in all its permutations. In this photograph a young man, my father, stands in the midst of his tobacco seedbeds, lord of all he surveys. Behind him black workers are watering the seedlings: an image emblematic of the old tobacco colonies—old Rhodesia, the southern states of America. With one hand this man cradles a baby girl, held close to his heart, while in the other he cradles a cigarette. You can just discern, and almost smell, the smoke wafting out of the picture. So much hope for the future envisaged in those tobacco seedlings, in that child. False hope, as it turned out, though had he lived longer he might have been proud of his daughter's capacity for absorption, her tenacious nurturing of certain infantile sensations and values. Not much surplus, however, in those values. Not all tobacco farms in old Rhodesia (and now in Zimbabwe) generated a profit, despite the supply of a large and cheap labor force. Each year anxiety would grow as the rains failed to come, or came at the wrong time; as the dreaded tobacco mosaic virus (a cigarette-like microbe that mockingly causes a disease in tobacco plants) invaded the crop; or as the auctions revealed a change in international fashions and last year's winning strain didn't raise an eyebrow, far less a living.

Instead of piss or vomit or crap there is only ash. In the smoking of tobacco we might say that nothing natural remains, but ash bears testimony to memory and the memorial aspect of smoking. Yet if smoking preserves, there is also an association between burning and the ruin of memory, a destructive aspect to the heat that rises up through the floor of the tobacco barn, to the flared match and the burning tip of the cigarette. Burning cigarettes (which are supposed by some to destroy the gray cells, the matter of memory) might be seen as akin to burning books. Book burning was inaugurated along with the introduction of the printing press: when Luther published en masse his inflammatory pamphlets, his Bible in German instead of Latin, he provoked retaliation—the books were burned. For some historians this conjunction of events offers an illuminating image, since they see in the coming of the printing press the beginning of the burning away of memory. In this scenario the invention of the press equals simultaneously the commodification and destruction of memory (since it was no longer necessary that people remember in the same way, for themselves). Similar arguments are made today about various forms of electronic data storage, particularly computers, which somewhat ironically are associated with the fact that the universe is running down, burning away, suffering terminally from "heat death." There is an example often given to illustrate entropy: when a computer records an item in its memory, the total amount of disorder in the universe increases—the increase of disorder (energy dissipated as heat) is greater than the increase in the order of the memory.

So if we are all running down, burning away, suffering terminally from "heat death," perhaps smokers are simply more entropic than most. While smoking may well be thought of as pure expenditure, the term also carries connotations of preservation. Just as smoking preserves fleshy foods—meat and fish—for future consumption, so tobacco smoking is also a way of preserving the past. In this instance, however, the past is not preserved, like a fish, as an object; rather it rises up, unexpectedly, as a fishy smell. The sensate "fish" summoned thus, through a kind of olfactory history, is real without being actual, ideal without being abstract.

NOT WANTING

∽

I do not want a cigarette.

To say this is terrifying. It's tantamount to saying: "I do not want."

To not-want: this is to be dead, or if not dead, then boring. Dead boring.

Yet sometimes I want, passionately, to not-want. Too much wanting kills. At times like this I want to forget.

I want a smoke.

BURIAL

∞

In the dead of night he is wakened by a strange sound, an animal-like scratching and scuffling just outside the bedroom door. Some wild creature sharpening its claws, shredding the carpet—though the muffled sound of heavy breathing is not like an animal. It is utterly and horribly human. He reaches out for her, but his arm moves in the dark through a vast and empty space. She isn't there. He is alone in the bed and there is something or someone strange in the house. In an instant he is rigid, deafened by the sound of his own heart. Eventually, after a long time, the house is quiet again, just the distant chugging of the fridge, the dog gently groaning in its sleep.

He is reassured by the sleeping dog, realizes he must have dreamed the alien sounds, dreamed into being fears long dormant. These fears, acquiring life, had turned on him like vengeful demons: unnerving, but not as bad as an intruder in the house. Better they assault just him, in his dreams, than his children. He thinks of the children sleeping, feels a sudden pain that softens into tenderness and slowly passes. Then, remembering that the children are children no longer, have not lived at home for years, he stretches, breathes deeply, and folds into sleep again. He drifts in and out, dozing for a while, enjoying the sensation of relief, a sense of reprieve after a false alarm, a close shave that brings you to the edge—even if only momentarily—of a precipice.

Suddenly a sharp and ugly sensation yanks him into wakefulness. He leaps up, finds himself crouching on the bed, ready to spring, go for the jugular. A sliver of light moves swiftly across the crack under the door. Silence. No gentle groans or somnolent growls, even the dog is silent. Or silenced. He anticipates a terrible almost-human howling, envisages Max Cady in *Cape Fear* prowling the house, passing through the walls like the holy ghost, invisible. He can feel the presence of a figure on the other side of the bedroom door, someone holding their breath, listening to the silence. His own eyes grow accustomed to the dark, although he cannot tell whether he is now seeing or feeling in the dark. The door handle moves, imperceptibly, hardly at all. No, not at all, it hasn't moved, he tells himself. But even as he tells himself this, he knows there is a man on the other side of the door, holding the door handle in one hand—turning it calmly, implacably, by minute degrees—while in the other he grips a knife smeared with canine blood. "He's coming for me, to slit my throat. And no one will know." In a flash he sees himself: pathetic, like some beleaguered beast, baring its throat to the butcher. Cautiously he slinks back under the covers. He will pretend to be asleep, but he is alert—he can see through the loose weave of the blanket—and will trap the intruder.

The door edges open and in the crack light flickers. A figure moves into the room, a dark silhouette.

The figure turns into the light and he sees: it is her. Only her, a figure as familiar as his own body. The tension begins to dissipate, but slowly, uneasily. It is as though knots have formed through his being from tip to toe. He holds his breath and watches as she moves across the room, easing the wardrobe door open, carefully trying to avoid the habitual squeak. I must oil the hinges, he thinks. With her back to the bed, shielding the flashlight beam, she scrambles among old clothes piled at the back of the wardrobe; she burrows into the bottom of voluminous coat pockets, turns shirts inside out, baggy jeans upside down. He knows that she will already have gone through the house searching in jars, behind books in the bookcase, at the back of untidy drawers filled with junk. It happens once a year or so: the evil spirit comes upon her in the night, and she invades her own house, excavating the accretions of daily living, wanting desperately to find a remnant of the past, a sign of life. "Not much to ask," she'd say if pushed, "a little thing."

That thing which is so simply and satisfyingly itself: a cigarette.

He pretends to be asleep, to not bear witness. And after a while he does drift off, but it is into a troubled dreaming he has fallen, as though her edginess has pervaded his sleep. When he wakes again several hours later, she is still not there. He gets out of bed and goes to draw the curtain to shut out the moonlight pouring into the room. But as he gets groggily out of bed, he realizes that earlier it was pitch-dark—there is no moon tonight. At the window he looks down and sees that the porch light is on, a floodlight illuminating a scene of ritual. She is on her knees under the big flowering eucalyptus, which drips redly in the harsh light, and she is digging. Around her are strewn hyacinths that have been ripped out of the earth. Her pale pink candlewick dressing gown is smeared with dirt and her hands, which she now lifts up in front of her face, are muddy.

What is she doing? Praying? Burying a body? Stashing some incriminating evidence in a safe place—her own front yard?

She is holding something in her hands, cradling some object, some precious mysterious thing. Which she now lays on the ground, unwraps the cloth that is wound around it, and tenderly wipes off the dirt with the hem of her dressing gown. Then it dawns on him: it is not a burial ceremony that has taken place in this clandestine theater, but a disinterment, a grave robbery.

SHE LOOKS at the object that fits so snugly in the palm of her hand. The cellophane wrapping remains intact, the contents will still be pristine, preserved all this time in their garden grave. Can she bring herself to do it, will she tear the wrapping?

She remembers, all those years ago going out, armed with a shovel, into the garden and digging a grave. A small grave, but deep. And in it she had buried a tiny coffin. Her last pack of cigarettes. In Smoke Stoppers they had told her: "Imagine the pack of cigarettes as a coffin, and all the cigarettes you've smoked as corpses." As a young teenager she'd had a boyfriend who'd said, "Kissing a smoker is like putting your tongue in a wet ashtray filled with cigarette stubs and ash. Or even worse," he'd said, warming to the horror, "it's like putting your tongue into a cremation urn—full of the ashes of a dead person." But these were not the injunctions and warnings that had provoked her private and elaborate rite; rather, she had done this in order to enact a ceremonial separation, to anchor the mourning, to stake the grieving process. Now she sees that this was a gesture bound to fail; rather than letting go, she had perfidiously conceived of this little coffin as a safety deposit box, a last resort, a final refuge. Yet how could it ever represent finality or be exhaustively symbolic? As she looks at this small pack, at once wondrous and pathetic, as she ponders the few cigarettes contained within it, the very fewness of them calls up the thousands, millions of cigarettes smoked in her lifetime. Is it the activity of smoking that is mourned, she now wonders, or the individual being of those cigarettes? She remembers a friend saying to her (or perhaps she had read it, the book on her pillow, the words entering consciousness as she fell asleep): "Smoking is like movie watching: often you can't put your finger on what it is that is so pleasurable about the images unfolding before your eyes, wrapping around you in the dark." Like cigarettes it is not the special taste or aroma, color or movement, narrative even, that produces pleasure, but that slight giddiness that springs from the *not quite the same* in which we recognize the *same* tobacco.

HE THINKS, as he watches: Like a dog, she is digging up and picking over old bones, looking for trouble, scratching open old wounds.

THE GRAVE is gouged out, amid the hyacinths, like a wound, and from this gash in the ground memories suppurate. She is watching as a coffin is lowered into a big black hole. There is a palpable sense of something escaping, swirling up, entwining the mourners, each of them lost in their own grief, reveries, and inappropriately profane reminiscences. All the smoke he'd inhaled seemed now to be expelled, to be returned as a gift or a curse, circling in the air.

It was her first husband's funeral, though he was by then no longer her husband—many years had passed since they'd smoked their last cigarette together, ritualistically marked the end according to the beginning, and the duration, the years of their youth. Arguing, cooking, writing, reading—one of them would put a cigarette, or a joint, down and the other would pick it up, just as their sentences, and their bodies, tangled together.

Then all of a sudden she had stopped smoking. Even at the time it had seemed a most peculiar and curiously unmotivated act. Where, she wonders now, had the idea come from: what thoughts of penance, heroic renunciation, childhood dares, sacrifices during Lent? Of course she had found it impossible to be herself-not-smoking and to be with him-smoking, and so she had taken herself away for a while to stay in a friend's apartment while the friend was overseas. Just after she had "given up" (the habit, as opposed to giving up on giving up, that would come later, though perhaps after all—she thinks now—that's when it had all begun) and moved out, the friend had returned, bringing her, as friends always did in those days, a carton of duty-free cigarettes. So as to avoid an appearance of ingratitude, she accepted the now unwelcome though highly tempting present and turned adversity into the occasion for a good deed: she made a trip home, leaving the carton as a gift for him, a kind of recompense, a substitution for her presence. Or so she thought at the time. Her absence and abstention, however, didn't last for long. Within a few weeks she was home and they finished the last few packs together. Now she wonders, perhaps her gesture of renunciation had been less about cigarettes and more about her need for him; her gift had been less a recompense and more like a reproach, a churlish defiance of dependency, a petty transference.

Later, after he had died of lung cancer, she stood by his grave and wondered: was it a gift I gave him—or poison? Was the giving of that gift actually an evil rather than a good deed? Or merely an inchoate petty thought made manifest? An evil deed would have been better; at least it would have about it a certain honesty, declaring itself: "Behold I am a disease." But a petty thought, as Zarathustra says, is like a fungus. "It creeps and stoops and does not want to be anywhere—until the whole body is rotten and withered with little fungi."

SHE DOESN'T TEAR the cellophane. Instead she takes a box of matches out of her dressing gown pocket and strikes a light. She holds the match up against the night sky for a moment and then brings it to the pack. It catches light, flares, and begins to burn. She drops it into the grave and watches until there is nothing left in the hole in the ground but a small mound of ashes.

HE WATCHES her from the window. She will return to bed and the next day will be pale and brittle and will talk of being bothered by nightmares she can't remember. And the day after that she'll be her old self again. This is something that happens; no matter how well he knows and loves her, he does not know what it is that happens when she enters her other world, and he cannot go there with her—into that accursed place.

LIKE A PRECIOUS GEM

∞

Men, women and children [smoke tobacco] indiscriminately, and are so fond
of its fumes that they inhale them not only at daytime, but also at night hang
small bags of tobacco around their necks like a precious gem.

O. F. VON DER GROEBEN, about the inhabitants of Sierra Leone, 1682–1683

23

Smoking in bed. Sharing a cigarette. Watching David Bowie
in *Merry Christmas, Mr. Lawrence*. This is heaven: the conver-
gence of bed, you, smoking, and David Bowie. Bowie, a prisoner of war, is in his cell awaiting execution. The guards come
to fetch him, but he makes them wait while he prepares for
the end. He picks up his hat, holding it upside down in the
palm of his hand like a bowl, and turns to the wall. Peering
into the wall as though into a mirror, he rubs his chin, dips an
imaginary shaving brush into the bowl, picks up an imaginary
razor, and begins to shave. Slowly, ritualistically, he mimes
the act of shaving and then of drinking a cup of tea, and then
he reaches out and takes an imaginary cigarette between his
fingers. My hand reaches out for the pack and starts shaking a
cigarette loose, but your fingers close around my wrist, and
you whisper, "Wait."

He inhales deeply, luxuriously, you can feel the nicotine
spreading through his being. And then he exhales, running
his tongue over his lips, tasting, catching a stray strand of tobacco. He savors that cigarette. When it is almost finished he
throws it to the ground—cut to a high-angle medium shot of
his boot stepping on the imaginary stub. Then he moves off,
out of frame.

After the movie is over we make love, smoke a cigarette together, inhaling before the altar of the television, giving thanks that we are not in prison. Lulled by the fumes we doze, the pack of Camels on the bedside table, within reach, like a precious gem.

A young man faces you, lurches forward, coming at you from out of the television screen. You can't easily discern his face as he stumbles forward through the smoke. He is wearing jeans, his chest bare, and all around him there is billowing acrid smoke. It smears his body, blurs his outline, stupefies. You have the sense of something in the background, out of the frame, a solid mass on fire—a burning house.

SHE IS IN TOKYO, watching the news on television, when this image suddenly appears. And out of the mysterious babble of a language foreign to her ears, a word rings out: a familiar word resounds, comes straight at her like an aural missile. It is the word *Yakandanda*, the name of her home, far away in Australia, where she lives in a weatherboard farmhouse with her son. Now she is here and he is there. The image of the faceless young man comes and goes in a flash, but the bush keeps burning, burns in a wild montage of flames and crackling brushwood and crashing trees.

The sound of burning timber is intense, the television sizzles, at any moment it will begin to melt. Cinders fly out from the small screen and smoke billows into the tatami-mat living room. Her skin is dusted in a fine coating of ash. On the television there is now an advertisement for cigarettes, for a brand called "Luna" but she has caught fire, is caught in those images that have now disappeared from the screen, from this small room, from the world.

FEELING THE PARTICLES of ash fall through the air, she looks around and finds herself in a city leached of color, drenched in poison. In the aftermath everything is slow, people are disfigured, they fall, everything falls, the city seems to be collapsing inward. Japanese voices are muted, fading, she can't quite hear.

SHE STARES at the screen, begins to chant, rocking to and fro—Loo-na, Loo-na, Loo-na. And then the names of other Japanese cigarette brands: Peace, Hope, Parliament, Echo, Just. The litany expands, from out of her childhood other names singsong into the present, a lullaby list, as soothing as grungy yellow ducks that float in the bath and teddy bears grown bald and tufty: Pall Mall, First Lord, Rothmans, Carlton, State Express 555, Springbok, Lucky Strike, Westminster, Gold Circle, Consulate, Matinée, Peter Stuyvesant, Gold Leaf, Royalty, Guards, Flag, Goldflake, Life, Stafford, Vogue, Avon, Texan.

Watching television in Japan, she sees the Australian bush going up in flames and the only word she can catch is *Yakandanda*.

She imagines the worst: the faceless figure as her son, the burning house out of view as her house. She imagines her marijuana plants going up in smoke, her manuscript and all her books burnt, the smell of singed feathers as the chooks try vainly to fly, the blue-tongue lizard breathing flames. But then she thinks, No, this is the melodrama of homesickness, the fear that home will disappear when you're not there, that you'll be forgotten, that there'll be no home to return to. No, she thinks, I'm just being visited by the past, by those fires of childhood on the tobacco farm in Africa . . .

As the flames disappear from the small screen, extinguished by advertisements, the crackle of twigs continues, the sound of brushwood catching fire as the tobacco seedbeds are set alight. This is how it begins: with the building of beds, after which branches and twigs and dry grass are laid over the ground, and then it is set fire to. It's a way of sterilizing the earth, but always it seems to her like an initiatory ceremony, the ushering in of the tobacco crop. She watches, warmed by the flames and filled with a kind of terror and awe, at this fire so supervised, yet threatening at any moment to tear out of control, whipped by the wind into a tornado.

The phone lines home are all busy. Home. Is home in Australia, where her son is, or Zimbabwe, where her childhood is? Or is home where her books are? In which case she is scattered, through space, across continents, in bits and pieces. A nomad.

But not a real nomad like the Aborigines, who traveled across the Australian continent with smoldering fire-sticks, burning as they went, cultivating fire rather than fearing it. The white men brought different sorts of fire-sticks—they were aimed at people, not the landscape, but the effect was indeed to change the landscape through changing the nomadic life of the Aborigines and their fire practices. As soon as you occupy the land, she thinks, as soon as you put down roots, plant cash crops, build homes out of bricks and mortar or chopped-down trees, once you stock dwellings with books, then you're asking for trouble, asking for the tinderbox to explode.

She sits by the phone, watching Japanese television, smoking cigarette after cigarette. Each time she lights a match, she holds it up and watches the flame flare and then contract, all its energy focused on consuming the tiny sliver of wood. The match turns black and withers, and only when the flame reaches her fingers, when she feels the pain, does she blow it out. It's a small ritual, an act of superstitious magic—as though by a slow burning and methodical control of this miniature fire, she can keep the larger conflagration at bay.

She imagines Africa burnt to a frazzle, stripped of grass and trees, remembers all the fires of her childhood, whipped up by the wind, racing through long brown grass, dry and brittle. Thick *bundu* would be transformed in a flash into a charred and smoking landscape. Seeing the smoke, farmers and farmworkers would come from miles around: hundreds of men—with branches beating back the flames and trucks carrying forty-four-gallon drums of water. Terror was in the air—rising from the sweaty bodies of the firefighters, from the animals running wildly, from the watchers—everyone was afraid that the fire would reach the thatched huts and houses or that it would encroach on the cultivated lands, consume the fields of tobacco, maize, *mazamban,* and the smaller peasant crops of maize through which would be scattered *mbanje.*

She has seen this image on television many times before, seen it on films, seen it spring from the pages of countless novels. It's true that this conflagration has never been named before as Yakandanda, never been so close to home, but nevertheless it's a generic image that recurs, summoning up the great Australian frontier, the hostility of the environment, the great gulf between man and nature. Even though we now know that the British use of fire—as a means by which the native bush could be replaced by an imported landscape—only provokes conflagrations far worse than in preinvasion days, it is too late to simply go back into the past. Nevertheless she feels herself slipping backward, far back, further than living memory: watching the television image, at once so remote and so close to home, she feels suddenly like Captain Cook approaching Australia. When they watched the fires burning along the shoreline of the continent, the early explorers and invaders were terrified and shocked by what appeared to them as thoughtless and wanton destruction. But in fact this burning was controlled; it had been carried out for generations with the precision and studied care of a ritual. Fires were controlled through attention to topography, the winds, old fires. The fauna and the flora coexisted with and were nurtured by Aboriginal fire regimes. In hunting, fires would be deployed to flush the kangaroos from cover so that they could be speared or netted, and then when the nutritious new grass appeared with the following rains, the emus and kangaroos would be attracted back.

When the great fires erupted in Africa, everyone feared for the tobacco crop, for the emerald green fields that sustained hope and fueled the economy, but a strong element of irony seared that fear subliminally. Tobacco itself burns. It's true that Africa is slowly being eroded, turned to desert, by the destruction of the *bundu*, the turning of trees into firewood by a population of poor people without other forms of fuel for cooking and lighting. But consider every tiny cigarette, each as it sits in an ashtray turning slowly to ash—its very existence, as well as its moment of death by cremation, is posited on a long history that begins with burning and continues in a smoldering manner. In the beginning there is the burning of the tobacco beds, but then later trees are again chopped down and turned into firewood to feed the furnaces in the barns where the tobacco is cured. After harvesting, the brilliant green leaves are tied in bunches onto sticks or long poles, and these poles are stacked in tiers in the barns, which are built of brick with roofs of corrugated iron. They are very tall, allowing for several tiers of sticks. To cure tobacco, the barn has to be artificially heated by means of steel flues set along the floor. Fuel, most commonly wood, is burned in outside furnaces and the hot gases circulate through the flues, which, acting as radiators, send currents of warm air rising through the spaces between the sticks of leaf. Curing takes about a week from start to finish, a week of intense and closely regulated burning, during which the temperature is raised a few degrees every four hours, and during which tons of trees are avidly consumed. The trees turn to ash and the green leaves turn to gold. Later when these leaves have been turned into cigarettes, millions more trees will be chopped down, cut up, whittled down, and burned as matches.

She lights another cigarette, holds the match up, and watches it turn black and wither away. She tries the phone again and listens as the line buzzes and burrs, as signals hopscotch through space. This time it rings. She inhales nicotine, holds her breath, wills an answer.

As she waits she doodles in the ashtray, using her cigarette to draw tracks and patterns in the ash. Ash disguises human scent, the scent of fear. This means that after a fire, after the conflagration has died down and the landscape cooled, smaller creatures—blue-tongue lizards, snakes, rodents—can be tracked, their movements traced in the ashes, their burrows exposed. Where traditional Aboriginal practices have survived, as with the Pintupi in the Gibson Desert, small mammals that have become extinct elsewhere on the continent have also survived. It seems that they have coexisted with a particular fire regime, that they have been in a sense husbanded by Aboriginal fire practices. Nomadic burnings represented a form of exchange: fire turned the land into a habitable environment for humans, and in turn humans took on the responsibility of sustaining (or farming) the land through fire.

At last he says, "Hello." He's relieved he doesn't have to break the news. Their house has been burned to the ground, her books are all gone, the marijuana plants are merely a memory of anticipated pleasure, the blue-tongue lizard that lived under the house has not survived. But her son is alive. He was far away when the fire broke out and blazed for hundreds of miles.

It was someone else she'd seen—at home in Yakandanda. She puts the phone down, exhales, and switches off the television. An image, however, persists: she sees through the smoke the blurred figure of a young man stumbling forward, his chest bare, his body charred.

THE BODY HAS

A MIND OF ITS OWN

The story goes like this: a woman with a notebook journeyed
to a distant land. By day and by night she traveled, through
rain and wind and snow, across mountains and deserts, until
she reached her faraway land—a strange land from whence
travelers seldom return. You might call her an anthropologist,
though this would be after the facts. You might call her a re
formed tourist, though this, too, would be retrospective. You
might call her a Smoker. She came to this land to live among
the people so that she might know their ways.

She was resolved to return, but only when the time was
ripe; until then she would give herself over to the strangeness
of this place and these people, she would relinquish her shib-
boleths, open her eyes and her heart. But for the sake of safety
she brought with her a talisman or fetish.

Some wear their fetish close to the heart or hidden deep in
a concealed pocket or secreted under the floorboards. Not
she, she understood the fetish as a sign, moreover as a fluid
sign, whose symbolic strength derived from its dual function
as both a private thing and as an object in circulation, signifying in a chain of reciprocity and exchange. From her study
of ancient and other cultures, she understood that the sacred
object—talisman or fetish—must be possessed of certain para-
doxical qualities: it must at once be separate and inseparable.
To part with it—to offer it up as a gift or sacrifice or item of
barter—would be simultaneously a way of ensuring perma-
nent possession. Her fetish was the cigarette. She had re-
searched these people for many years before setting out on

her journey, and this she knew: they were renowned both for their primitive proclivities in indulgence—drinking and smoking—and their courtesy, particularly toward strangers. The cigarette would be her passport and her protection.

She got the idea, or perhaps she stole it, not from fieldwork manuals but from someone she met at a party who told her about George Orwell's anecdote that is also a practical instruction of how to survive when down-and-out in the great metropolitan capitals of the Western world: Orwell told of how he would regularly go to parties with only one cigarette in his pack. He'd pull it out and make an offer. "Have a smoke," he'd say, and the other person would reply, "Oh no, I can't smoke your last cigarette; have one of mine." Thus he would get through the whole party and go home with one last cigarette—either to smoke in bed or to put aside for the next party.

So when she arrived in her faraway place, our woman with her cigarette and her notebook, she made her way through the marketplace to a pub. For a while she observed the local customs and realized that no one talks, or listens, without a pledge of faith. "My shout!" she declared experimentally. The chorus went up: "Thanks, mate!" and suddenly the crowd around her grew, friends and informants materialized like magic. It was incumbent upon her, she realized, to put her money where her mouth was, and so she bought a round of beers—a very large round. Thus her purse was emptied. But perhaps it was worth it: tongues loosened, stories and jokes flowed, within no time at all she felt as though she belonged—party to intimacies, witness to indiscretions. After a while she pulled out her crumpled pack containing the single and singular cigarette, and offered it to the man next to her. "Oh no!" he said. "Couldn't take your last cigarette!" "No worries," she said, as she'd heard others around her say. "Oh well, then, if you insist," he said. "Thanks, mate." She watched him, animated by casual greed, take the cigarette, place it between his lips and lean toward her, waiting for a light. She obliged, and as she flicked her lighter, something inside her ignited: a malevolent hunger was born. Cigaretteless, she watched him smoke, slowly, taking great gulps of beer in between inhaling. Her fetish physically gone, her raison d'être in tatters, she experienced the beginning of a lonely craving.

She remained in the pub for several hours, and everyone around her seemed to be smoking and drinking in a cozy reciprocal fashion, but no one, after this, offered her a cigarette or a drink. Moneyless and alone, she felt her farness from home, felt the foolishness of her professional detachment. Her act had rebounded: instead of securing her a place (from which to speak and write), it had ejected her to the margins, distinctly an outsider. A craving outsider. Prior to this she had smoked in a moderate fashion—when socializing, after a meal, when writing in her notebook. She could go long stretches without smoking. But now for the first time she experienced a terrible craving and a terrible loneliness. It was humiliating—to be at the mercy of the weed, and so she determined to give up smoking, to rid herself of this dependency, to wipe the slate clean.

In order to not smoke, she resolved to stop going to pubs and into other public places, to stop going to barbies and to the beach, to refrain from participating in all such social rituals. She would last a few days and then crack and go out and buy a pack at her local corner shop. And every time she did this—every time she handed over her coins—she felt a loss, was pierced by the memory of talismanic failure. Instead of entering into the thick of social life, she began to hover on the edges, illicitly picking up scraps of food and conversation. She would cover vast tracts of the city by bus and train, arcane forms of transport in this city where the motor car reigned supreme; and on the buses and in the trains, she would listen in on strangers' exchanges. But she found it harder and harder to write in her notebook, and the harder she found it, the more tenaciously she clung to her notebook. When she was tempted beyond endurance to smoke, she would clutch her notebook close to her heart and mutter an incantation.

One day she woke up and realized that renunciation alone was not enough; she had to cure herself through immersion in other forms of ritual, practices of healing peculiar to this place, so faraway, even now or perhaps especially now that she was there, living in the vicinity, speaking the language. And so she put away her notebook and resolved to enter proactively, as the locals put it, into a campaign of self-healing.

FIRST SHE GOES to the ashram on the hill. Here she parks her car in a leafy suburban street, unlatches the Hansel-and-Gretel gate in a white picket fence, and enters a messy vacant lot, overgrown with weeds and stinging nettles and tall grass. Fighting her way through this wasteland, she emerges into a luxuriant, haphazardly planted garden: pumpkin vines trail through flower beds; climbing roses are entangled with green beans; spiky aspidistras bloom among the cabbages. Monkish people in orange and pink robes are festooned around the garden, lolling on the lawn, their limbs entwined, some in pairs, some in larger groups, stroking and licking one another or passing joints, and even ordinary cigarettes, from mouth to mouth. The monkish ones always eye her lasciviously as she walks by, sometimes offering her a smoke, causing her heart to palpitate. She scuttles quickly through the mass of bodies and miasma of smoke, through mingled smells of patchouli and marijuana. Inside the spacious hall she feels immediately calmed. The roof is high and thatched, the rafters built from old railway sleepers, once-mighty jarrah trees, the tallest of the forest trees. She unfolds her mat, closes her eyes, breathes deeply, and listens to the instructor intone: "Feel your breath, feel your breath wind through you, winding through you like an *S*, feel your breath like love, winding through you. *S* for *Self*, learn to love yourself—*Self* with a capital *S*." Absorbing this mantra, she feels that, through yoga, she might indeed transcend the body and as a sort of compensation be blessed by love. Until one session when the instructor elaborates on his theme: "Feel your breath winding through you, winding through you like an *S*, massaging your inner organs," and an image of Mr. Leopold Bloom comes into her mind, eating with relish the inner organs of beasts and fowls. Smells fill the air, and the rubbery, mushy textures of thick giblet soup, nutty gizzards, stuffed roast heart, liver slices fried with bread crumbs, and, above all, that thing Leopold Bloom liked most: "grilled mutton kidneys which gave to his palate a fine tang of faintly scented urine."

IT WAS IMPOSSIBLE to return to the ashram on the hill. Instead she went to a Chinese doctor, who comforted her craving by providing her, at great expense, with innumerable small packets filled with mysteriously named herbs. At home in her smoke-free kitchen, she boiled the dingy flaking herbs, khaki colored and foul smelling. At first she was overcome by the malodor, and so she started writing again in her notebook, recording the sensation, the strangeness. But before too long she felt her nostrils tickled by a floating tuft of memory. Through the herbal stench there wafted a fine tang teasing her palate.

And so it was that she spent all the money she had saved for acupuncture on a solitary feast composed of the inner organs of beasts and fowls and a pack of unfiltered Camels.

Restored, she ventured out into the world again and—pen poised, notebook on her lap—began initiating conversations. But as soon as she opened her mouth, people looked at her in mute bewilderment, and so she grew dejected and began to mutter to herself. A kindly stranger took her by the hand and led her to a house in the suburbs that was also a medical practice.

SHE AND THE weary despondent doctor look at each other across the vast expanse of his almost-empty desk. "I could give you Prozac," he says, "but this is no cure for being friendless."

"It's not the friends I miss," she says. "It's the cigarettes."

His eyes light up, he springs forward in his chair, clasps his hands together purposefully, lifts a framed photograph that has been lying facedown on the desk. The glass is dusty and the image is slightly out of focus, but it looks like a little girl and a Labrador dog and something missing; the photograph has been torn, someone ripped out of the scene.

"Now here's a problem I can help you with," he says cheerfully. "This is something we can cure."

She looks back at him, dubious.

"I'm a hypnotist!" he declares. "Western medicine is all very well, but it can't do everything. In fact, between you and me, it has let us down." He begins to slump again. "Out there, there's a waiting room full of people who think I'm going to cure them."

"Little do they know," she says, "you bring them the plague."

At this he flashes her a grin, boyish and buoyant, and for the first time she notices his eyes—twinkling blue, like delphiniums. "Exactly! You've got it! But you we can cure. Hypnosis. Five sessions and you'll never want to smoke again, your alienation will evaporate, your depression will be whisked away."

"And have you always been a hypnotist?"

"Oh no, for a long time I was just depressed. Like you. But a doctor, a depressed doctor. Then I met a hypnotist—actually he came to see me about his kidneys and we got chatting and he suggested retraining. I was horrified of course; all those years invested. But you don't have to give up medicine he told me—it has its uses, for kidneys and the like. Just think of hypnosis as a supplement to your armature of cures."

"And now you've retrained?"

"Now I've retrained. Just received my diploma. You could be my first success story!"

You got your training from a man with troublesome kidneys, she thinks, and odors drift into the office, comforting odors, of livers and kidneys and stale cigarettes, and so she thinks, Oh well, might as well give it a go, might cheer him up, who knows.

So she settles into the lumpy old donkey-textured armchair and tries to concentrate, to enter into the spirit of the enterprise, to match his fervor. To demonstrate her commitment to self-help, she pulls out her half-smoked pack of Marlboro Lights and drops it into the bin filled with stained swabs and crumpled sodden tissues dropped by weeping patients. Incredulity bubbles up when he brings out a pocket watch and starts swinging it, but she swallows her incipient giggles and swivels her eyes to and fro, to and fro. At last he stops the swinging and starts intoning. "Look into my eyes," he commands, and she obeys, luxuriating in their blueness, sinking like the dormouse into a comforting bed of delphiniums blue and geraniums red. "When you leave here, you will have no desire to smoke, no desire at all, no desire to smoke." He begins his speech in a monotone, aiming his injunctions insidiously, worming his way into her lazy unconscious, but as his words start flowing and warming, a zealous cadence begins to shape his speech. "You will look at cigarettes and feel sick, you will want to vomit, you will never smoke again."

Afterward, having "woken" her from the hypnotic trance, he offers her, like Prince Charming bearing the glass slipper on a satin cushion, a cigarette. He looks so expectant, his desire for affirmation so craven, that she quells her instinct to reach out and take the poisoned offering. "Ugh, no, no thank you," she says, pulling a frightful face as though the very thought fills her with nausea. The sight of her frightfulness fills him with pleasure—his own face lights up; he glows like a Halloween lantern.

SHE LEFT the house in the suburbs that was also a medical practice, and that had just become a hypnotic center, and as she walked away, she delved into the inner reaches of her shoulder bag, feeling for the packet of Drum that always nestled there. She rolled a cigarette and inhaled deeply, nicotine breath winding through her, winding through her like an *S*, massaging her inner organs.

Massage, she remembered someone saying, massage is the best thing for restoring bodily well-being and balance, for eradicating ill humors and haunting smells, for obliterating the fine tang of faintly scented urine and stale tobacco. So she looked in the Yellow Pages, where she found it hard to distinguish between massage parlors and masseurs in either the archaic or the New Age sense. She finally opted for the most alluring name: B. B. King.

"CALL ME BRUCE," he says. He is a very large man with hammy hands and a square squashed pugilist's face. "Call me Bruce," he says, stubbing out his cigarette in an overflowing ashtray. He pours baby oil into the palms of his hands, rubbing them together. "Fee, fi, fo, fum, you're in for a treat, love, we'll have you out of here a new person. You can relax now, you made it through the lions' den, we can both relax, in here's a haven; my aunties—those old harridans—won't let me smoke in the house, here it's heaven, I can smoke and you cannot smoke. Well, you can if you want to, but I think you'll like my massage more. Relax, love, you're safe with me."

She wonders.

Given a choice she'd have stayed in the lions' den. B. B. King, it turned out, also lived in a leafy suburban street, though the leaves on his street were less dappled and the lawns a little more straggly. She had been greeted at the front door by two little old Scottish ladies, who had ushered her into a genteel old-fashioned front parlor. They sat her down in a deep maroon wing-backed chair, offered her tea, and engaged her in conversation. The wallpaper was delicately baroque: naked cupids flying through space, blowing trumpets wreathed in garlands of lilac and purple. There were framed prints on the walls—of the Blue Boy, and Highland Cattle, and Leaping Salmon. On the many French-polished occasional tables were arranged framed photographs of family and family pets. In the past and in a foreign country, this room would have been reserved for entertaining guests, she realized. But here there were no guests, only clients come to visit their nephew, the masseur. Ingeniously, they had turned the room into a threshold between worlds, a liminal zone, where they presided as keepers of the flame and the books. After tea and conversation, you were asked to pay your fee, your name would be entered in an exercise book, and a receipt would be written out in copperplate. Then they would usher you—one on each side—through the threshold, and you would pass into the hallowed area of the massage room, a closed-in back veranda, fibro walls, looking out on to a bare backyard.

SHE IS LYING on her stomach, his hands moving over her back. Her head is turned on its side, and she is looking at a print of a rodeo tacked to the fibro wall. There's a flurry of dust, a bucking horse, a man riding the horse as though he were riding the crest of a wave. A wave in the dusty outback. She sees that it is signed by a well-known artist. "Lucky you," she says to Bruce. "How come you scored this?"

"Well, that's me, the skinny bloke on the horse. Put on a few pounds 'round the kidneys since then."

"But you're a masseur."

"In another life I was a rodeo rider. Had a bit of a name, actually, in the outback. Go out back of Bourke and any bloke'll tell you about B. B. King. In those days you could give me a horse, any horse, wild and woolly, and I'd ride it, stick like a fly to shit."

"So how come you became a masseur?"

"Not such a leap, you know. It's all a question of balance, rhythm, understanding the body, muscles, not just the outside but the inside, too; you gotta have a feeling for the inner organs—of beasts and fowls and humans."

Only now does she realize that her body has been in spasm,

muscles clenched. As anxiety oozes out, serenity enters her being. He doesn't look like a magic man, but he is. He has magic hands.

"Take these hands. They have a life of their own. They have a gift for healing. And where do you think this gift comes from?"

He pauses, waiting for an answer. She hopes he does not expect her to say God.

"Look at these hands." He crouches down in front of her. They look to her like a butcher's hands. "Amazon hands, that's what they are. I never knew where it came from, this gift, these hands that can heal. Then one day I saw this book of Minoan sculptures. Look I'll show you." He disappears for a few minutes and then comes back. "Tell you what, why don't you sit up, put your top back on, and we'll have a cuppa and a smoko and look at these pictures." He disappears again and she can hear him communing with the aunties, and he returns shortly with two mugs of strong tea. No fragile teacups and saucers this time.

He hoists himself up onto the bed and there they sit, side by side, looking at the pictures. "They were a matriarchal culture you know," he says. "Amazons. Look at these sculptures, look at the sinew and the muscles; they understood the body. So when I saw these pictures, then a little red light went on in my head, and I understood. In another life, long ago, long before the rodeo riding, yours truly was a Minoan, an Amazon."

"Bruce," she says, "I want to give you something." She reaches into her bag and pulls out a crumpled pack containing a single and singular cigarette. "Have a smoke."

"Oh no, I can't smoke your last cigarette, have one of mine."

"Oh thank you, thank you, I'd love to. But you are meant to be curing me of smoking."

"And so I am," he says, "All in good time. Trust me, listen to your body, the body has a mind of its own."

And so they drank their tea and smoked and she felt contented.

WHITE MAN

⌒

It may be taken, to avoid useless repetition, as a general rule that whenever a civilized person has intercourse with a native of this country the latter begs tobacco. THOMAS BAINES, *Journal of Residence in Africa 1842–53*

The savage is hopelessly prone to addiction. Correlatively, addiction—characterized by lack of willpower, responsibility, and ethical consciousness—is an index of the primitive. We know this from early explorers, adventurers, and invaders in southern Africa who tell endless tales of how addicted the Africans or Kafirs were, how—in the thrall of addiction—they would shamelessly trade magnificent cattle, women, anything for a plug of tobacco.

The whites responded to this exercise of primitive desire by using tobacco as a trading item: "The Hollanders gradually advance into the country which they buy up with tobacco," says the Abbé De Niro Choisy, who stopped at the Cape in 1685. But occasionally we get an inadvertent insight into white dependence on the weed, as in a book called *How We Made Rhodesia* when the author, in the course of a tirade against the trade monopoly exercised by the Bechuanaland Trading Association, writes:

> To illustrate the rapidity and extraordinary profits at which sales are effected, 80,000 cigarettes, Virginia Bright's, were sold in less than an hour and a-half, realising over £300, i.e. from £3 15s. to £4 a thousand; and more striking still, some of these were retailed, by those who were lucky enough to secure them in the first instance at about 8s. a hundred, at 2s. 6d. per packet of 10, and I know that later

on, when the supplies were running short, one single cigarette fetched the enormous price of a shilling.

Sitting in the archives in Harare now, pouring over these musty documents, what seems most obvious is that it is the white man who is obsessed with tobacco, and indeed not without reason, because tobacco is crucially identified with the project of invasion and later colonialism. These early documents read as superb instances of projection, arcane evidence of the process by which tobacco—so closely identified with the savage—was to become the medium by which Rhodesia entered the international monetary community, was to become synonymous with white Rhodesia, with the colonial enterprise. In the teens one of the most popular Rhodesian cigarettes was a brand called "Old Cannon," the name derived from the Gardner machine gun deployed during the first Chimurenga (liberation struggle) in 1896. It stood until after independence in 1980 mounted on a pedestal on Main Street, Bulawayo, dedicated to the memory of the 259 "pioneers" who lost their lives in the rebellion. Ironically a brand of cigarettes is used to epitomize the power of colonial rule; in fact an analogy is forged between the white man and tobacco.

There are of course other ways of describing and imagining the early use of tobacco in Africa. Some of the reports, as is always the case in the best anthropology and travel writing, vividly evoke a range of smoking practices that are inventive, elaborately social, and intriguingly different from familiar Western customs. Sometimes these "other" uses are adopted or even emulated by Europeans, and occasionally homage is even paid in the form of acknowledged borrowing. In France in the seventeenth century, a group of officers were in the habit of meeting together regularly and smoking and talking after dinner. One day one of them who had spent much time in Africa proposed that they smoke African style from one pipe—a very large bowl was perforated in several places and ten or twelve tubes were inserted into these holes, permitting as many persons to smoke simultaneously. The officers constituted themselves as an order, with fifty rules outlined in a pamphlet published in 1683: *Institution et statut de l'ordre des chevaliers de la cajote* (*cajote* being the African name for this pipe).

AT THE HEART of the movie *Dead Man* there is a joke about tobacco. Nobody (Gary Farmer), the hero of *Dead Man*, is a renegade Native American who travels out West with a character called William Blake (Johnny Depp) and who knows more about the poet William Blake and his poetry than Blake does himself. As they travel through the reservations Nobody is constantly trying to buy tobacco and is constantly refused, although the traders are more than happy to sell to William Blake. Blake is slowly dying, and at the end of the movie Nobody enters a longhouse and persuades the elders of the tribe to give him a sea canoe in which Blake sets sail toward his death. Nobody gives Blake a twist of tobacco—which he (Nobody) has spent the whole movie trying to secure—to take with him into the future. The last line of the movie is Blake saying, "But Nobody, I don't smoke." Jim Jarmusch has said that this joke is for indigenous American people: "I hope the last line of the film . . . will be like a hilarious joke to them: 'Oh man, this white man still doesn't get it.'"

ANOTHER WAY of looking at the early use of tobacco in Africa is to focus on the white man from the perspective of the "savage." The picture painted by primitive art is often not a pretty one, so that cigarettes, cigars, and pipes are often given an iconic status along with guns and drink—to suggest either indolence or domination. In a book called *The Savage Hits Back*, there is a reproduction of a carved ivory tusk from Lourenço Marques (now Maputo, capital of Mozambique) that came to the National Museum of Copenhagen about 1880. Various scenes are depicted in a spiral formation, scenes that delineate native reactions to the coming of the white merchant. In the lowest section, slaves—their heads shaved and wearing the slave halter—are joined together by a heavy chain around their necks. The next panel, in contrast, shows men who are carrying on a pole a huge and beautifully carved fish—either taking it to deliver to their employer, the white merchant, or to sell to him. On the top panel the merchant himself sits on a chair, with his dog at his feet and his tobacco pipe in his mouth. While labor and servitude are enacted around him he, the exploiter, obliviously indulges his propensity for indolence.

I wonder what the picture will look like in a few centuries' time, how the picture of our culture will be configured. Who, I wonder, will be subjected to mimetic mockery and caricature, where will projection be located? Will it be the smokers in their ghettos and glasshouses and underground lairs who seem to be so abject and socially irresponsible? Or will researchers of the everyday wonder, in the future, why so much scorn was heaped on tobacco smoking in the fin de siècle, why this quotidian habit attracted so much moral vehemence. What was at stake, they might wonder, in these intricate patterns of projection?

TRANSLATION

(a gift of opium)

Lurid yellow letters lick the orange cover of a tiny paper-back—*Au Feu du Jour* by Annie Leclerc. On the desk next to this book there is a dull dark blue, almost black book, a huge French-English dictionary. On top of the dictionary sits a white pocket-sized edition of *Opium* by Jean Cocteau.

I read a minuscule bit of *Au Feu du Jour* each day, a paragraph or two. I read fetishistically, looking up every word in the dictionary, even the words I know, compelled to get it right. I write down the translation, word for word, amend it, scrawl a line through the verbiage. Begin again. Each day begins this way, a torturous regime yet somehow salving. I want or need this discipline, this ludicrous ritual, which if nothing else produces writing and therefore a modicum of comfort, albeit writing that is only mimetic, and crudely so, always only approximate. It's as though I need this activity of translation in order to come to grips with something incomprehensible, something that is utterly familiar as an experience, as sensation, but that, as knowledge is inaccessible, foreign. I need to know exactly about this smoking business. But exactitude eludes me; this knowledge has to be filtered, deciphered, unearthed, traced out.

The Book of the Dead in Sri Lanka, a gigantic tablet inscribed in stone. I remember reading this book: mysterious, hieroglyphic, ephemeral.

Some mornings I cannot manage the massiveness of these words, their obdurate massing together, the hostility of their stonewalling. There is nothing to write. Then I flick through

Opium and look with wonder at Cocteau's drawings. He sketched this text, words and drawings, while in a detox clinic (between December 1928 and April 1929). Some of his drawings are demented: lines shoot off in all directions, disconnecting and transposing parts of the body, shattering all solidity. Mostly the body is figured as a surface punctured all over by orifices and peripheries; and from every orifice pipes, curious funnel-like tubes, issue forth. One of the most lucid drawings, sketched with cartoon clarity, shows a hand—palm upward—nonchalantly cradling both a sharpened pencil and a cigarette, its tip weighted with ash. This drawing fills me with delight. Is it recognition merely, or is it that these lines on a page perform some kind of sympathetic magic, enact some sense I cannot put into words, but that I sense nevertheless—as a lightening of the body? As a smile?

WHEN SHE WAS packing up to return to Lebanon, Lina left me a pile of French books, mostly novels, and her French-English dictionary. As a special gift she passed on to me *Opium*. On the title page of *Opium* are two inscriptions, one in pencil and in French, almost faded, and the other in red ink. The first is from Sophie to Lina, a memento of the "old life" to take with her from her homeland to Australia. The second is from Lina to me, and it says: "If I give you this book that is precious to me, it is because I know it is in good hands. Maggie said that Colette said that it is only worthwhile giving something that is precious."

Little was she to know then *how* precious; how one day, rather than holding a cigarette or a pencil, I would hold this little book in my hands and laugh.

NOW LINA WRITES to me from Beirut—her mother is dying, amid carnage and bombs and flying mortar lodged in her back—but the doctors say it is not from carnage that she is dying, but from lung cancer that they discover when they dig the mortar out of her flesh. Her mother is a vegetarian and has never smoked. "My mother's body," Lina writes, "is laid out, on the table, and the doctors are writing the story of this body, even though she isn't yet dead and we can hear the sound of bombs exploding and buildings crumbling. I scream at them to put away their pens and scalpels, but this old man in a bloodstained coat says to me, 'The bombs are outside. Inside, life goes on.'"

In a P.S. she adds, "People die just as much despite health as because of illness."

This postscript is like an afterthought, like a strand of smoke, a gift wending its way between the past and future, her and me, life and death. It is a gift laced with poison.

IT IS MONUMENTAL, *made of stone, the Book of the Dead. You can't curl up in bed and read it, or send it through the mail, inscribed in pencil. You cannot hold it in the palm of your hand, and hand it on to someone else. Yet something circulates as you—a foreigner, a tourist—walk slowly around this granite scripture. Something you cannot put your finger on, even though you can reach out and touch the chiseled surface.*

Smoke rings lock in the air, hieroglyphs, entangled gifts. You put your hand out to touch and it closes around nothing. Yet when you open your hand, something, before you know it, escapes and proceeds toward a destination.

NO SUBSTITUTE

"You know what this is like?"

No, I don't know what this is like. It's like nothing else except other times the same, unspeakable.

"It's like . . ."

I wait. He looks sideways, fleetingly, as though to catch my eye. I dodge. His glance veers, slips its tether, disappears. I slither out of focus. Calmer here in the smudginess, calmer than in the concentration of his wanting. He wants complicity. He wants me to agree. He thinks, or hopes, there are words to say it. After all this time he doesn't know: there is no approximation.

We sit side by side, eyes downcast. Words unspoken circle, settle in our laps. Like gifts, overprotected, tarnished by fondling. Like . . .

"Like what?" I say.

He doesn't look at me. So now I turn, out of the haze, and watch his face. There's a tightening; it's as though the liminal years, years of capricious gratification, are being gathered in, as though the residue itself were here and now distilled: the clarity of aching. His face, it's as though . . .

"It's like," he says, "like you're lying in bed with a woman you really love, really I mean, and you've just had your first big row. And you lie there not touching. And you just don't know, this might be the end—you're lying next to this woman you crave and you're not touching and you know you might never touch again.

"Know what I mean?"

He expects me to understand. And I do. The piercing accuracy of this stab in the dark takes my breath away, my mind off other things. For a moment.

Half an hour to go. We've been flying for three and a half hours, observing all prohibitions. Strangers strung out together. All we have in common is that it feels like this plane ride will last a thousand and one nights. Our lives depend on keeping open options, so what we make of each other requires ingenuity. We've been generous, lacing our confessions, understanding both of us that what matters now is difference, not sympathy, that what each other needs is something shocking: to pass the time, divert the craving. We act out of character again and again, fishing for incredulity. Each time he says, "know what I mean?" it's my cue for disbelief, a provocation to knowledge more arcane, more tenuous, less likely.

We are both, then, taken aback by a moment of understanding less contractual, more primitive. But the moment passes. He chuckles. "I'll stop soon. No problems. Done it before. After all, I'm forty now, time to moderate my habits."

A simile is no substitute.

∽

Stranded.

In the middle of nowhere. The desert stretches, flat and red, in all directions. It's all the same, everywhere she looks it's all the same. For two days and two nights she's been traveling by bus across the continent. Now she stands and watches as the bus moves away, faster and faster, leaving her behind. Red dust swirls and hangs in the air for a few long moments, obscuring all movement, and then the cloud subsides but still the bus moves, so fast that soon it seems to cease movement altogether.

"Call me," he'd said, "call me when you make a desert stop." "No," she'd said, "there'll be no stopping, no turning back. When I get on that bus I'll go, and go, and then I'll be gone. Forever." She could have left quickly, caught a plane, been somewhere else before the day was over. But she needed time, time to endure the implacability of space, time for her body to tell the difference. This is what she wanted: to arrive at a point where she could say with conviction, "Here is not there. You are over, there. I am here." Once she'd crossed the continent overland, lived through every tedious moment of a desert crossing, it should be possible to not look back, to not call home. This is what she'd believed, or vehemently hoped, when she'd packed her bag and caught that bus.

She'd only turned her back for a moment. But in that moment the bus had gone.

In the early morning they'd pulled into a small haphazard desert town. Hardly a town really, scarcely a settlement, just a few gas bowsers, a couple of prefab constructions, a scattering of cars—some rusting into the landscape, a few with their hoods up as though awaiting repair, or perhaps just waiting. And on the edge of town a couple of large formless mounds. As the bus had approached in the dusky light of dawn, these mounds had loomed out of the low flat landscape, imposing and monumental. For a moment it had seemed as though they were in a black-and-white movie, riding on horseback into Monument Valley, riding to the rhythm of *My Darling Clementine*. But as they'd drawn closer and the sky became lighter, it had become apparent that these monuments were in fact garbage heaps, composed of tin and metal shards, brightly colored duco fragments, shredded mag wheels, tattered remnants of upholstery, leopard skin, and scarlet vinyl—smatterings of urban decay tossed into the wilderness.

All desert towns seem unsettled, but this place had seemed particularly impermanent. Everything was in a state of suspended animation, only half complete, or incomplete; it had been impossible to tell whether buildings were being demolished or built. The women's toilet was in a portable hut surrounded by rubble in the middle of a desultory construction site. It was like stumbling into the past, restaging childhood trips at night to the dunny at the end of the yard, tripping over tricycles and dogs bones and empty beer bottles. Before going in she'd leaned against this Port-a-Loo, feeling the dawn dissolve behind her eyes and the heat rise up through the ground, up through her body. She'd watched as a teenage boy had filled the bus with petrol. He'd climbed onto a forty-four-gallon drum next to the archaic bowser and pumped by hand; even from a distance you could see the sweat drip from his face. In the toilet she'd dozed for a moment and then rubbed her eyes, tried to focus on the scrawlings and carvings all around her, tried to pull some sense out of the teeming mass of ideographs. At last a phrase had loomed up out of the scriptural frenzy. "Institutions," she read, "are the graveyards of desire." Then she'd come out into the day and already it seemed hotter, lighter, and through the glass tube you could see the pink liquid in the bowser slowly disappear as though evaporating into the haze.

There was a whirl of red dust spiraling slowly in the dense light, and then the dust settled and she saw her bus disappearing.

She watches as it recedes, moving pneumatically, sucked smoothly into the distance. She watches as the road narrows, becoming a line, and the bus contracts, becoming a point. Just a point moving over a line. Then for a long drawn-out moment the point seems frozen, a dot suspended in space. She imagines reaching out into the haze, detaching the dot from the line, her fist closing around it. Then she would hold that bus in her hand. It seems so simple—to stretch out your hand and retrieve what's lost. But the void in her stomach tells her this: movement is *in* the bus, along with your flask of coffee, sleeping tablets, money, bottle of scotch, baby pillow, beta-blockers, and the thriller you're halfway through, whose ending you can't live without.

Movement is in the bus and movement is in her body. She feels her body moving away from her. Stranded. As though she were a fish landed in the desert. A sensation of sickness overwhelms her; she is seasick—on dry land.

When there is nothing left to see, she turns her back on the desert and flings open the fly-wire door of the roadhouse. "It's gone! The bus is gone!" she announces loudly. "I'm stranded!"

The roadhouse, which has no windows, seems to have been assembled from the inside out, constructed and inhabited by slow degrees, as building items have randomly materialized—bits of pink fibro, planks from packing crates, concrete bricks. In one corner a discarded though still greasy engine of a combine harvester leans against a stack of tins labeled ORGANIC INSECTICIDE—UNSAFE FOR HUMAN CONSUMPTION. In the center is a large Formica-topped table. The faded ocher-and-brown pattern of the Formica, intricately veined with detritus, gives an appearance of bilious marble. Around the table are yellow and orange plastic chairs, and despite the lack of purposeful design, it is as though there is an echoing of the exterior world in the interior of this roadhouse, a pale pastiche of "desert tones." On the dusky pink linoleum floor, between the doorway and the table, there's a piece of brown cardboard, torn raggedly from a box, on which is scrawled WET PAINT. She sniffs, to catch the pungency of paint, but there is only the smell—and sensation—of dust, even the sign itself is dusty. Lolling on the plastic chairs are a few pale androgynous teenagers, who turn and look at her vacantly.

"The bus has left me! I'm stranded!"

No one says anything. All you can hear is the sound of an ancient fridge chugging interminably. Disbelief and cold horror flood through her, as a premonition, vague but sinister, takes shape in her stomach. An intimation of immortality, a vision of life in this place going on forever and ever, no escape. This is it.

And then a voice speaks. "Sit down, relax, I'll make you a cup of chamomile tea." The voice is solicitous, hazily familiar, and utterly improbable. She turns and there behind the counter is someone she knew once and never expected to see again. Back in the city she and Maggie had met in a hypnotic state. They were both enrolled in a "Quit the Natural Way" program, and through their spectacular failure, their tenacious resistance to the grain of the hypnotist's voice, had formed a brief and intense alliance. Now Maggie leans nonchalantly on the counter as though this is what she's been expecting, this is what she is here for—to make chamomile tea for old acquaintances stranded in the desert. On the wall behind her there are racks of dusty cigarette packs, every imaginable brand of cigarette is there, including those that are obsolete and those that are foreign: from Indonesia there are small packs, red and scratchy gold with an elephant motif and a memory trace of exotic odors, and there is a huge selection from Japan, each pack scripturally dense, crammed with hieroglyphs and names in English—names like Peace, Hope, Parliament, Luna, Echo, Just.

"I'll make you a cup of chamomile tea," Maggie says now.

"Make it Lipton's," she says. "Strong."

On the counter there are heaps of knickknacks, curios, souvenirs—as though someone has upended a Santa Claus sack and tipped all the exotic contents out prior to sorting and stacking. But no one has ever gotten around to the second stage, and the jumble has settled into a sort of sculptural complacency. She extracts a longish object shaped rather like an old-fashioned fountain pen and blows the dust away to reveal a toothbrush, the handle of which contains some murky liquid in which a minute koala jerkily climbs a tree. As it reaches the top, you turn the toothbrush to tackle those plaque-infested back molars and the little koala goes crashing down to the bottom of the tree. As she lifts a garishly painted plastic boomerang, the paint immediately starts flaking, falling in slivers to the floor. There is lots of fishing tackle strewn around, and an assortment of flies, and a box full of little domes that you shake till they fill with snow and you can vaguely discern a goldfish wafting. She cradles one of these in her hand, shakes it, and then holds it to her ear as though she expects to hear the ocean echoing. She imagines lying with Jack, her head on his chest, the beating of his heart passing through her body. If you bought one of these knickknacks as a memento, took it home, and put it on the mantelpiece, what would you be commemorating, she wonders. What way is this to remember a desert town? And yet she feels a strong compulsion to buy this curiosity, to preserve within it the sharpness of the sensation that has just passed through her. But she is penniless—all her money is on the bus, speeding across the continent. Moreover, she's renounced the past, packed her bags and said good-bye. Yet to forget entirely would be too ostentatiously evasive, she thinks now, a casual act of cowardice. She would like to embalm her memories, like goldfish in a dome on the mantelpiece, so she could shake them up at will rather than be at their mercy.

She wonders: If to be homesick is to be sick from a craving for home, then shouldn't seasick mean to be sick from a craving for the sea?

Maggie returns with a tray and they sit down together at the makeshift table. The silent teenagers slink away, disappear out the door into the vastness. She lifts the mug of hot tea and lowers her head. Steam rises up, engulfing her face, assuaging the dryness of her skin. She sips, the taste reminds her, a craving stirs, tentacles spread with the liquid heat through to her fingertips. An opened pack of Camel cigarettes lies on the table. In the background a woman's voice emanates from the transistor:

> *I'm tired of these small-town boys,*
> *They don't move fast enough*
> *I'm gonna find me one who wears a leather jacket*
> *And likes his livin' rough.*

Her fingers flex, she reaches out, and then stops, puts her hand flat on the table, feeling like a child submitting to nail inspection. "Well," says Maggie, "there's not much else to do in the desert. So I smoke."

"Well," she replies, "not me, not anymore. When I got on the bus I left all that behind."

"And now the bus has gone," says Maggie.

They drink their tea. Maggie smokes a Camel and asks, "So how's the city?"

The city, she thinks, what is there to say of that city except that he's there and I'm here. He saved me once—from small-town boys and restoration drama, and still he's there, in that overgrown town, in Pygmy City, where everything converges, where everyone shares, where innuendo always reaches further than its destination. She remembers arriving there. She was taken for a Sunday drive, through the suburbs and then through dense forests in a park famous for its natural vegetation. They stopped at the edge of the park where there was sloping lawn and you could sit on the grass and look out over the river below and see the sights of the city. Corporate toy town. All around them people were admiring the view and assiduously setting up barbecues. There was the smell of eucalyptus and burning flesh. "It's a great place to bring up kids," said the husband. "The air's so clean." This was a refrain that would come to haunt her on sleepless chlorine-suffused nights. "It's a great place to bring up kids!" On this first sightseeing expedition she took a deep breath to put them at their ease, demonstrate her willingness to assimilate. She imagined her body a voluptuous vacuum cleaner, pumping and sucking, in unison with all those other Sunday afternoon bodies sucking and pumping, sucking and pumping, innocently deployed in the service of some superbly economic civil ecology. She reached into her pocket, pulled out a pack of Camel cigarettes, which she handed around. "Thank you," said the wife, "we don't smoke. But please, feel free."

The sensation of domestic renovation creeps under her skin, the sound of seamless couples chanting "we" "we" "we" all the way home. She remembers floors stripped bare and polished like small-town brides, the smell of chlorine wafting up and out of swimming pools, saturating the atmosphere. You'd catch a sudden whiff in nightclubs at three in the morning; you'd go to the library and pick up a book, and breathe in chlorine. The retribution of inertia. She was trapped in a haze of chlorine fumes, and then he materialized: illicit, driven, contemptuous.

Not exactly a breath of fresh air, but once she'd had a taste of him she wanted more, needed more . . .

She'd said she wouldn't call—"When I get on that bus there'll be no stopping." But now the bus has gone, leaving her with a sensation of seasickness.

When Maggie disappears to find out, via the two-way radio, whether there are any more buses coming through, she wanders over to the far end of the counter where there is a dusty display of paperbacks. She pokes around in the fishing tackle and finds a hunting hat to use as a duster. Beneath the hat is an antique black telephone, elegantly inlaid with gilt. Out of curiosity she lifts the receiver and is surprised to hear a dial tone. She puts the receiver down. As she dusts and browses, an unexpected treasure house of reading emerges, scrupulously sorted and labeled according to genre. WAR and ROMANCE make up the largest sections. First she scans the titles cataloged under ROMANCE: *Sweet Captivity, Desperado, The Wings of the Dove, Fugitive Heart, Seduction, The Barbarous Touch, The Wolf Man, Emma and the Flying Doctor.* Then she fetches a chair and settles in to read some of the dust jackets in the WAR section: "From the Gallant Few who held on to the bitter end came the battle cry that rocked the world" (*Alamo Nights*) and "They were men of men, and their fathers were men before them" (*Shaka the Zulu*). Then she fetches Maggie's pack of Camel cigarettes and box of matches, takes out a match, and starts chewing as she peruses the most innovative section—THE DESERT. Here she finds *Nemesis, Veiled Threat, Bad Night at Oleander Oasis, Terror's Long Memory, A Reason for Being, Partners in Grime, Children of the Desert.* Flipping through the introduction to this last book, she picks up the receiver and begins dialing. While the number rings she reads: "A psychoanalyst sits in his office and receives patients who want to be cured. An anthropologist goes to some tribe in the desert or jungle and tries to understand those people— who certainly do not want to be cured, indeed, they could teach us a lesson in happiness." A voice says, "Hello." She lights a cigarette and takes a deep breath.

Regret rises in her throat as he says, "Tell me you miss me."

"I miss you."

"Lie to me—tell me you love me."

"I love you."

"Tell me you'll never leave me."

"Do you want me to come home?"

"Do I want you to come home? Look at it this way, seems you've got two choices—you can stay there, like in the middle of nowhere, or you can come home."

"Or I can keep going. Depends on the next bus, where it comes from, east or west . . . where it's heading."

"How about we do it this way. I'll ask you a riddle and if you know the answer you come home. But if you don't know you keep going."

"OK, ask me a riddle."

"There's this hunter, right? And he's after this bear, pursues it a mile south, then a mile west, and then finally, at last, a mile north. At this point he shoots it. When the bear is dead the hunter looks around and discovers that he's exactly back where he started. Now the big question is . . . wait for it . . . what color is the bear?"

It's a trick question and she knows the answer—he had told her long ago, the first time they had woken up together in the morning. Half asleep, feeling curiously safe she'd murmured, nuzzling, "My shaggy bear."

"I'll tell you a story about a bear," he'd said. "Once upon a time there was a bear and this bear was being chased by a hunter . . ." The story unfolded lazily, words rising languidly out of the dreamtime. But when he reached the end his voice was sprightly, poised to spring back, like a steel trap. "What color is the bear?"

The bear, then and now, is white. "The trick," he'd told her then, "is you have to think about where in the world could this hunter's journey—a kind of triangle—take place. Obviously it has to take place at the North Pole. If you start at the North Pole there's only one way you can go—south. You just have to think about north and south as directions along lines of longitude, and east and west as plus and minus along lines of latitude."

It's a trick question, in more ways than one. He knows she knows the answer and asks the question in order to lure her home. But she knows that for those who answer riddles, home is a dangerous place to be.

"See if you can answer this one," she says. "There are two trains on a single track, moving, from opposite directions, toward each other. One is filled with drunkards, the other with Norwegians. The trains don't ever collide. Why?"

"I'll think about it," he says. "You can tell me the answer when I see you."

She wonders if he says this because he wants her, her presence, or if he says it merely in order to deprive her of the punch line. She tells him, "Because Norse is Norse and Soused is Soused and ne'er the twain shall meet."

"I'm not good at this you know, it's hard for me, but I'm doing my best, can't you hear it in my voice, I'm begging you for Christ's sake—I'm on my telephonic knees."

She smiles, charmed again by his way with words. Once, one would have said "his way with women." But in a more self-conscious, telephonic age, the distinction is blurred. She knows that no one anymore says, "I can't live without you." To make such a declaration would be merely to flaunt naive duplicity, and this he knows. His sentiment is presented raw but tossed in irony—so as the words are passed from mouth to mouth tastes mutate, dissolve on the tongue, deviate from certainty. It disturbs and excites her that she can never tell, with assurance, whether he's serious or sardonic. His habitually parodic rendering of romance—is it a warning, a declaration that romance *is* redundant, unoriginal, a mere enactment of cultural tropes? An anachronistic matter, of matadors and bleeding hearts and suitors on padded knees? If this is so, does she then exist only as a figure of speech, to be always mocked—for getting it wrong, reading too much into a situation, a gesture, an intonation? Or is this affectation of irony not a warning but an invitation, a sign of something deeper, of emotion too strong for words? So he offers up a cliché, but is careful to encase it wryly in quotation marks, thus inciting her to decipher something more authentic, more personal, meant just for her. These elaborate maneuvers—if she laughs in his face he's well protected, can always claim a prior lack of seriousness—touch her in a way she can't quite grasp, perhaps because they so precariously camouflage a tender, and surprising, impulse.

"I'm down on my telephonic knees"—words that sound like the lyrics for a pop song zing over the wires, instantly connecting desert and oceanic suburbia. She hears a murmuring: "I can't live without you." She feels his hands move over her, a warmth in her belly, his mouth between her legs. I can't give him up; I can't live here in the interior, alone, apart.

She forgets all the other partings. The time he'd pushed her face away, violently, grabbed bits of clothing, and clutching his shoes and socks announced, "If I don't go now I'll never go." He'd walked away, barefoot, from her house. Leaving the door wide open. She forgets the tirades, accusations hurled at her body like paint against a wall. Phrases of love fondled, suggestively, as offerings are fondled—but always on the verge of separation. She forgets all the times she'd returned, responding to the hotness of his words, only to be met by a blank expression, a nonchalant turning of the back, a cool ferocity. She forgets there is no home. As such.

"I'll tell you what," she says, and it takes all her nerve to say it, to make up her mind, "I'll take a gamble. If the first bus that comes along is heading home, I'll see you soon. But if it's going the other way, then . . . I'll call you . . . when I get there." He says, "You think there's a logic to escape, a congruence of time and motion and place." She thinks: how much latitude does a shaggy white bear need?

Maggie returns with some items of sustenance—a vial of valerian tablets, a jar of Tiger's Balm to ease the stress, and some of her own books: *Confessions of Zeno* and *Ten Thousand Light-Years from Home*. "And here's something else, if you want it, it's yours—I'm quitting"—a pristine pack of Camel cigarettes.

"No need for sacrifice."

"No worries."

"Well thanks . . . just till I reach the other side."

Standing outside the roadhouse, she looks to right and left, to east and west, and wonders from where the bus will come.

Oh, my bête noir, my shaggy bear, my never-ending story. What next?

SCREAMING

∽

Later, there was screaming.

I think that often it's like this: the screaming comes later.
And lasts longer than you could ever imagine. Sounds unut-
terable, screamed into the landscape.

She was on a train traveling through Africa. The journey
went on and on, and through the window nothing changed.
Everything was brown and indefinite. In the train, people
were playing cards, drinking, smoking. After several nights,
and days that blurred into a smoky haze, a fight broke out.
Without warning. But once it began it was there forever. At
first you could only hear the noise, sounds of bodies falling,
ricocheting down the narrow corridor, sharp edges absorbed
and muffled by the haze. A man stumbled; quickly we pulled
the glass door shut, just as he fell toward us, thudding, a heavy,
almost inert mass of truculence. Deflected, his body lurched
across the door, smearing the glass with blood.

The train kept going, its rhythm never broken. We stopped
talking, played cards in silence, smoked in slow-motion. It was
several hours before we reached a town, and then the train
stopped.

It was nowhere. A pale pink fibro hut and a long low platform in the middle of the desert. The train stopped and we
leaned out of the windows, but all we could breathe was the
heat. Our mouths were dry, particles of dust scratched our
eyes. Before us a scene unfolded in silence. The body was carried off the train, wrapped in white government-issue sheets,
swaddled like a gigantic molested baby. Cops dressed in khaki
were waiting on the platform with handcuffs held out like an
offering. Small black children appeared waving curios—

bright lucky bean bangles and calabashes carved for tourists. The murderer was escorted off the train, and a woman and two young children followed after. She was empty-handed, but the children trailed a tartan cardboard suitcase and a couple of bright plastic pails and spades for digging in the sand beside the sea. They stood there, a mute tableau on the platform, desert all around.

They were motionless. The air was hot and still. Then out of the silence came a scream, a razor-ravaged wailing. The dust settled in the air. And the scream hung there.

I CALLED and left a story, a desert story, on your answering machine, and at the end of the story I screamed. I wanted you to hear it as it was in the desert. You took this story, took my voice, and turned it into radio, but you used another scream, someone else's furious wailing. I took umbrage, slighted by this act of sonic substitution. Your response seemed, on the face of it, reasonable enough. You said, "Your scream got cut off—at the very point where the scream began building, the tape ran out. What could I do? I didn't want to sacrifice the story. I searched the archives, though, till I found a scream that matched. No one would know it wasn't your voice." We joked, on the telephone, about the purloined scream. Of course I thought you thought my scream wasn't up to scratch.

Instead of screaming *at him* she turns the scream into a gift; instead of accepting the gift he turns it into an affront; instead of her scream he uses someone else's scream; instead of walking away she lights up another cigarette. And practices screaming.

TO BUBBLE AND RUMBLE

(like an elephant)

∞

One thing leads to another, say the prophets of pestilence. But what they mean, these tinsel-tasseled prophets—whose pronouncements, all wrapped up and beribboned like birthday gifts, are delivered with glee—is this: they mean that one vice engenders another, far worse than the first, and so the rolling stone rolls, gathering vice like lice, toward a sticky end.

As teenagers caught smoking, we were warned that next it would be *dagga*, and then hard spirits and hard drugs, and then before we knew it we'd find ourselves perpetually stoned, rolling down the yellow brick road toward perdition.

Most commonly our elders would deliver their pronouncements over sundowners, relaxing at the end of a day spent out in the tobacco fields, stretching out on the veranda, where drinks would materialize silently, brought on a tray by a black servant. It was a social hour, a time for swapping stories, hazarding opinions, talking politics, exchanging gossip. A congenial, communal time, before too much was drunk and tempers frayed and accusations were made. Tobacco boxes would be strewn around, the old boxes of thirty, there for the taking, to be shared. It was patriotic, and considered sociable too, to smoke. It was a way of supporting the commodity they produced, and moreover cigarettes were dirt cheap.

Today, in Zimbabwe, cigarettes, as elsewhere in the world, are not so cheap. In the high-density suburbs of Harare, the black youth are more likely to cut their teeth on *mbanje*, which is very cheap, much much cheaper than when we were young (in those days our elders never, to our knowledge, smoked *dagga*, as we called it; though among Africans it was traditionally the case that only elderly men were allowed to smoke the weed). Though of course even today it sells for a considerably higher price in the low-density or middle-class areas, and no doubt it was the case then too.

BACK IN ZIMBABWE in 1997 she goes with her lifelong friend, Maggie, to a benefit concert for Oliver Mtukudzi and the Black Spirits—three members of the band had died the previous year from AIDS. The Bundu Boys were in the lineup, a big attraction, yet only one of the original six remained alive to play that night. Everyone at the concert would have been touched, probably closely, by death. That day she and Maggie had made a flying visit to the bush, to sit for a while by the Shawanhowe River, after years of drought flowing fast and brown and splashing over low flat rocks. Out on the Mtoko road, turning off to Saint Paul's Mission at the little cluster of shops at Mudumbu General Store, a sign flashed past, a blur at the time but imprinted on the retina, coming into focus as an afterimage: a rough sign, handpainted in large letters on cardboard—COFFINS FOR SALE. The crowd at the concert was predominantly middle-aged and middle class, racially mixed, inclined to melancholia and nostalgia. Nevertheless there was a defiant energy, a vibrancy in the air. She and Maggie bumped into Bob, with whom they had been at university. She has no memory of this graying overweight man, but Maggie says to her, "Yes, you do remember: he always played the second spear holder, and in *Richard II* he spat over the front of the stage, and he was probably a Tick Bird." She has managed to block out of consciousness the existence of the Tick Birds—that whole gang of rugger-bugger beer-swilling avowedly racist white boys. They took their name from those large white birds that sit on the backs of cattle, picking off and eating ticks—big, gray, and swollen with blood. The Tick Birds thought of themselves as constituting a club, not a gang. They had a tie pin (with the Tick Bird emblem) and a mission: to prevent the black parasites from growing too fat on the backs of the whites. Their methods were crudely vigilante: people who stepped out of line—by crossing the color bar and sleeping in the wrong bed, for instance—would be beaten up. Tonight, nearly thirty years later, Bob is here with his black friend who holds a senior executive position with a multinational tobacco company. Bob is puffed up with success through association. We reminisce on safe ground, recalling the exotic drugs of old. "Remember," he urges us, "remember the fabled Malawi Gold and Malawi Black. Man, that was magic stuff, man that would transport you somewhere else. When you could get it, that is, scarce as hen's teeth, and cost a fortune! For years and years we all thought it was the real thing, this Malawi stuff, and only years later do we find out we were suckers—it was all a fantasy, probably grown in a backyard down the road in Mount Pleasant."

"But in the sixties," someone says, "it wasn't a fantasy, it was real."

IN THE Golden Corridor and the Beira Corridor in Mbari, the oldest township in Harare, you need to be tough and to have at your disposal that invaluable commodity street lingo, and you need, if you value your life, to be in a youth gang. For these are heavy drug-dealing areas, compacted urban versions of the larger geographic zones of production and exchange. Mostly the youth smoke *mbanje*, and then sometimes move on to cigarettes—but the progression does not indicate a causal chain, a rolling stone gathering incremental addiction and vicious momentum. Cigarettes, in this context, perform a red-herring function: they are smoked primarily in order to hide the smell of marijuana. Their success—in achieving a state of odorous red herringness—is in fact dubious; but actually there is something more at stake than either serial olfactory substitution or proliferating drug dependency. The relation between cigarettes and *mbanje*—at once real and imaginary—serves to delineate a map of social relationships, to activate a ritualistic zone of exchange. Gangs are formed through rituals, and conversely smoking rituals are invented, practiced, and refined through gang living. In Mbari it is the custom for everyone in a gang to contribute money toward the purchase of a twist of *mbanje*, and everyone has to participate in smoking it. The reefer circulates and when it reaches you, you take a few puffs and then pass it on to your neighbor. You trust people to be equitable, but even if you suspect that someone is being greedy, you do not draw attention to this, and to pass judgment is considered very bad form. When it comes to cigarette smoking, the protocols are still designed around and through the formation of the gang as a kind of party animal, but both the "dancing" and the "democratic participation" are enacted differentially. A gang or group will normally buy one cigarette and "cut" it—to be smoked between four or five members. The "cut" here is metaphorical since to actually cut the cigarette up—as one might a pie, for instance—would be to rob it of its very essence, its smokability. Metaphorical it might be, but the imaginary cut performs a material function. Before commencing, the group works out together how much each person's cut is—that is to say, what length of the cigarette may be smoked. Then the ritual begins, the cigarette is lit by the first person, who proceeds to smoke, precisely, their portion—no more, no less. If you refuse to cut appropriately, you might expect to find yourself in big trouble. On the whole, the cigarette culture is less scrupulous about gang membership, though there are still inviolate customs: it's more generally the case, for instance, that if a stranger approaches, you *must* cut; but, on the other hand, groups can be formed on a contingent basis—for the simple and sole purpose, say, of smoking a cigarette.

It is mainly boys who belong to gangs, but there are some girls who gain membership as honorary boys—not exactly through the performance of bold, adventurous, and tough acts, but rather through smoking *mbanje*, which attests to their boyish ideality, to their possession of those qualities that constitute being a boy: boldness, toughness, an adventurous spirit. They seldom, however, smoke cigarettes.

PERHAPS ONE could say that it is the traditional custom of the male elders smoking *mbanje* that has led to the youth gangs and their smoking, and likewise that it is the phenomenon of the male youth smoking that has led to an unprecedented situation of girls smoking. One thing leading to another, one little stone beginning to roll, propelled on a vice-and-lice gathering trajectory. And nowadays it would no doubt add fuel to the fire of the demonic antismoking evangelists to have evidence that the smoking of marijuana leads to that noxious drug tobacco. But in fact the chain of causality is a lot more tangled and the distinctions a lot more blurred: distinctions, for instance, between addictive drugs and legitimate medicine, male and female, old and young, between different recreational substances. Which is not to say that there are no differences, but rather that habits and rituals change, boundaries are redrawn, patterns of reciprocity mutate. And the reasons are rarely intrinsic to the substance or to the category.

Nowadays, for instance, the idea of tobacco as poison is presumed as common knowledge. But not so long ago tobacco, in certain countries like England, was used as a medicinal substance to cure a variety of ailments, including coughs and colds (and in parts of Africa it is still used today to counteract asthma). By all accounts it worked as well as any contemporary cures for these same ailments. A vestige of this "superstition" persists (the obverse of the belief that tobacco inevitably kills) in the United States in the current preoccupation with all things "natural," manifested nicotinely in a brand of cigarettes called "Natural American Spirit," which is marketed as whole-leaf, natural tobacco, 100 percent free of chemical additives. The pack features a Native American chief smoking a long pipe, a primitive promise of peace.

Or take the idea that it was traditionally only the male elders who smoked. Among the Tonga, a matrilineal people who lived (until forcibly relocated because of the building of Lake Kariba in the 1960s) on the banks of the Zambezi, it was women who were the big smokers. Even today it is women, and only women, who smoke an elaborate calabash pipe called a *nefuko*, the gourd of which is half filled with water, with a clay tobacco-holding bowl placed above the ball of the calabash, while the long, gracefully curved stem is used as a mouthpiece. The bowl and the calabash are connected by a reed that reaches into the water-holding gourd. Once the bowl is loaded with a layer of tobacco and a layer of crushed millet or sorghum, a glowing coal is placed on top of the mixture to get it burning, and a cone made out of corrugated iron is set on top of the bowl as a windguard, its shape resembling the steep pitched roofs of the Tonga houses. The smoke is filtered and cooled by passing through water in a similar manner to the hookah: smoke is drawn down the reed tube into the calabash, where it bubbles up through the water into the stem and into the smoker's mouth. Smokers in action, so it is said, can be heard a long way off, making a loud noise very much like the rumbling of elephants.

The women, because of their apparent exoticism, occupy center stage in most accounts of the Tonga, but in a preanthropological universe, David Livingstone saw only sexless (or now we'd say nongendered) smokers on the lower banks of the Zambezi. No doubt he only saw what was visible to white male missionary eyes, but he offers an anecdote that attests to the persistently inventive relation to smoking among all of the Tonga: "Large quantities of tobacco are raised on the lower bank of the Zambezi during the winter months, and the people are perhaps the most inveterate smokers in the world. The pipe is seldom out of their mouths, and they are as polite smokers as any ever met within a railway carriage." He tells of how, whenever they came with presents, they politely asked if there would be any objection to them smoking. "They think that they have invented an improved method for smoking," writes Livingstone, which he then proceeds to describe for the benefit of those who are fond of the weed at home:

> They take a whiff, puff out the grosser smoke, then, by a sudden inhalation contrive to catch and swallow, as they say, the real essence, the very spirit of the tobacco . . . which in the ordinary way is entirely lost.

The spirit of tobacco lives on among the Tonga through another substance—today they (men and women) are, in the popular imagination, renowned not as tobacco smokers, but for their cultivation and smoking of *mbanje*, and it is the one place in Zimbabwe where, supposedly, this common drug is in effect, though not in fact, legal.

Perhaps we have here a clear instance of the vice-gathering rolling stone: tobacco leading inexorably to harder drugs, to more lethal addictions, to the abandonment of all distinctions and sense of propriety. Yet, of course, it is very likely that tobacco and *mbanje* were always mixed: in precolonial times both plants grew wild and also were cultivated; both were smoked—sometimes actually mixed together in the bowl, and other times their differential usages marked out in ritualistic ways.

This is certainly true in many Western countries now, where in fact there has been a curious reversal in the hierarchy of demonizations. Where the prophets of pestilence once warned us of the slippery slide from tobacco to *dagga*, now the fear for many renounced smokers is that even a puff of marijuana—since it is probably mixed with a little tobacco—might act as a lethal hook, and before you know it you'll be back in the arms of addiction, back in a tentacled nicotine embrace. There is a solution for many: to smoke only *pure* marijuana. Others, who experience their relation to pure nicotine as therapeutic, not addictive (and who locate the addictive component within the artificiality of cigarettes, within the impurities accumulated in processing), are able to reconcile their dilemma by smoking "Natural American Spirit."

LONGINGLY she recalls the famed Malawi Gold, how they would save and savor this marijuana so superior to your run-of-the-mill product, she remembers long druggy and drowsy afternoons, lovers long gone. She knows that she can never again smoke marijuana—not primarily because of its association with nicotine or even because it contains a smidgen of tobacco, but because it is still a cigarette, and once she puts it between her lips, inhales and slowly exhales smoke, once she does that she's a goner, another sacrifice to bodily memory.

The trick is to find a substitute, but one that instead of duplicating desire, articulates desire differently. If she belonged to a gang, a smoking gang, this might be possible, but she is too old now for the youth gangs and not enough of a man for the good fellas. She thinks about the current Tick Birds, keeping the body politic clean, consuming all tobacco traces, erasing tobacco desire. And she yearns for a different sociality. She thinks of the Tonga women and their *nefuko* pipes.

Up until at least the 1930s all Tonga women upon reaching puberty had their front teeth top and bottom pulled so that the stem of the calabash could fit into the gap left by the missing teeth. The custom, now considered barbaric, is dying out, but many girls still have the upper four teeth extracted in order to fully enjoy smoking the *nefuko*. If those Viennese psychoanalysts are right, she thinks, and speech is just a compensation or substitute for the first loss—the loss of that Edenic preteething state, devoted to gummy and sucking pleasures—then smoking the *nefuko* is less a substitute than an original pleasure. But for her it might be the perfect substitute; she imagines the pleasure of this intricate form of smoke inhalation, and she basks in the deferred but greedily anticipated pleasure of never having to speak again, merely to bubble and rumble like an elephant.

MEMORY MISSILES

She didn't always drink. So much.

She's lying on the floor in a bathroom, the tiles cool on her cheek. This coolness is intense, focuses all the night's melodrama in an icy obliterating blast. Her body feels at once too much—messy, oozing; and all angular—elbows and shinbones jammed into corners. She is very ill, wants to die. It's not so much the all-consuming nausea that she wants to escape—it's this image of herself. Repellent yet insubstantial, not a real image. More like an afterimage, a bit of leftover iconography from the jagged edges of martyrdom. She sobs, feels a jarring in her body but hears only this: a cruel bathetic parody of operatic anguish.

She remembers fragments from the evening. Shards of humiliation fly back in her face. She closes her eyes, grimaces, tries through an act of will to propel these memory missiles into space. But they fly back, they sting.

She remembers beating her fists on his door, berserk, furious. Screaming at him through the walls as though her fury could bring him out of hiding. The first few words she'd shrieked were incoherent, strangled in flight, but slowly they began to soar, incandescent curses shooting through the night. Each shot of abuse projected into space loops back into her veins till she is flying high on fury. Eventually exhausted she sinks to the ground. Slumped against his door outside in the cold, she sucks on a whiskey bottle, immersed in the texture of glass and burning liquid. She will drink herself into oblivion so when he returns in the early hours of the morning he will stumble over her. Just as he is about to enter his house, he will stumble on a body, fall and cut his head. No accident that she is lying there, a lethal snare, on the threshold. Not like a bride—no, she will not be carried over. Over and done with she'll lie there, dead drunk, his fatal flaw, his final downfall. Their limbs entangled, they will lie together. She will be pale as an imitation. He will be red, bleeding to death from the gash in his forehead.

He will bleed onto the rug in the hallway and his blood will run in rivulets through the house, staining the wooden floors, seeping osmotically into the furniture, into the library of books. Pages will stick together, favorite pages, passages underlined in pencil, asterisked, lovingly responded to around the edges, in the margins. Pages to be read and read again. No more. She imagines the dog cowering in a corner, shivering as it watches the bloody rivulets creep closer. The dog that used to bark at her as she crept up to look through the windows, to spy on him in the dead of night. The rivulets creep over its paws, spreading up and over, enfolding the creature in a coating of blood that shimmers and dries. It sits there—demure, like a chocolate dog in a shopwindow. She sees the other woman: in the kitchen stirring a pot of spaghetti sauce. As she stirs the sauce it thickens, seems to take on a life of its own. An obscure object, large and awkward, thrashes lethargically around in the liquid like a fish gasping for air. She plunges her hands in, gropes for the object. His heart. She clutches it to her breast, but it slips and slithers, flops to the floor and skids across the shiny parquet tiles. She stands there, his blood on her hands, and is turned to stone.

The house is almost saturated. Only one room remains. A pristine corner of a piece of sodden blotting paper. This room is the haven, there where the holy grail, the impeccable computer, resides. It squats, inviolate, bloated on memory. On the memory of her. That's all she is now: memory. Maybe not even that—maybe all that's in the memory bank are digits, arcane mathematical formulas, budgets, bookkeeping systems, income and expenditure, so much money made in solving problems, so much spent on furnishings and renovation. The conceptual nuances of domesticity. Inscribing the ideal home. Regardless, the tide of blood flows, flows in a fatalistic current like dirty dishwater to its destiny: down the drain. Into the computer it flows, permeating disks, contaminating, obliterating memory.

Lying on the bathroom floor, the thought of blood turns her stomach. Her body heaves. The smell of offal—hearts and entrails, braised brain and stewing tongue—invades the bathroom. She retches, again, and again. Till the lining of her stomach is stripped bare, there is nothing solid there, nothing material, and yet the memory image persists. She can't throw it up. She thinks of a room she once looked at in Scotland. The winter was bleak and she thought she would be warmer if she lived in a small space, cooked and wrote and slept and turned in circles like a dog anticipating the luxury of dreamtime. So she answered an advertisement: space for rent. But when she stepped in, she felt herself shrinking as though the room itself, besieged by desolation, were contracting. It was bare, the walls papered in a paisley pattern of fading brown and mauve. There was an air of ugliness in this room, of forced fading. All signs of life had been erased, the papered walls scrubbed and bleached and worn away, yet something ghastly in the pattern persisted.

Cheek pressing against the cold tiles, she finds herself again on his doorstep. Sucking on an empty bottle resentment surges; rushing through her system, it converts to energy—pure, irrepressible, like the arrow of time. Clutching the bottle, she crouches like a discus thrower, brings her arm back, and then propels her whole being into the air, hurling the bottle so that it flies, carving a rift through space. As it flies, obscene invectives bolt like bullets from her mouth. The euphoria of vengeance. Impact of glass on glass. As the crescendo reverberates her body staggers. The sound of tinkling, slow-motion. She hears an emptiness inside. It dawns on her that perhaps he is not resisting, holding out against her presence; perhaps he is simply not there. The humiliation of hating, passionately, a man who isn't even there.

She knows only one thing. She knows what she wants: she wants a cigarette. She wants a cigarette, and then she wants to die.

Lying now with her ear against the cold tiles, it's as though she is listening to a seashell and can hear her voice breaking, a torrent of words crashing onto the shore. A savage garrulous sobbing. In the opera when you know, with an intense pleasure, that things can only get worse, you also know that there's no telling, exactly, how things will turn out. What thrills is the reverberation—in the body—of the voice, of words *as* music, detached from sense. Voice touches somewhere where words can't reach. But operatic babble can also render resonance as pure banality. She winces, remembering how profligate she'd been, how she'd had to eat her words, how once inside her, they groped and clawed and forced regurgitation. Now that she's vomited everything out, she is still gripped by their deadly phantasmatic groping. If she lifts her head, she is in that wintry room in Scotland, spinning.

She lies very still and remembers that there was a time when she didn't drink. In Siena that spring, watching the early morning light play over dusty red buildings, leaning against the bar, dunking lusciously warm white bread into thick steamy coffee. Afterward, tossing back a small whiskey and as the burning sensation lingered in her chest lighting up a cigarette, inhaling deeply. Contentment, beginning the day, a ritual of precipitation. One drink didn't lead to another. She'd pay for her breakfast and buy a pack of Camels. Then she'd fill her flask with fresh cool water and head off to spend a day in the hills.

Now: no drink, no camel. Will she survive the desert journey?

A SMOKY EDIFICE

(implosion)

⌒

It's a delicate balance. The way this body hangs together strung out on some hypothetical framework, sometimes called a skeleton. It feels to me, though, this matter I inhabit, it feels boneless. Not a Cartesian body, to be drawn and quartered, balanced by weights and measures. I imagine skeins of nicotine, sinuous threads of smoke woven through this matter, holding it all together. Organs infiltrated and protected. See the lungs as crocheted intricately, matter folded, padded with layerings of tar, every tissue permeated by a mystery silkiness. This matter that is the body exists as an elaborate crenellation, resilient, pliant. Like wrought-iron lacework, this twirling smoky edifice is strong, able to bear any amount of stress.

In Los Angeles there exists a wondrous folly that isn't a house and isn't a sculpture and is hardly a structure. They call it the Watts Towers. A man named Simon Rodia built these towers all alone, obsessively over twenty-five years, next to the railway line in Watts, where black people live. The world heard about Watts in the sixties—the Watts Riots. Rodia built a series of towers that have no function, no interior space. The surface is an endless mosaic of permutating textures and colors; embedded in every inch of surface are fragments of glass, tiles, bottle tops, china. Whatever he found, day by day, he used. The towers link up in unexpectedly intricate and apparently random designs. They seem so fragile. The story goes that one day Simon Rodia stopped working and walked away, so then the city council started to pull down this weird edifice. But the towers were resistant—he had reinforced his concrete, his spindly crenellations were inviolable.

My body, over long years of smoking, has endured, built up an immunity. All this random messy matter coheres, is held together by spindly threads and tensile towers of nicotine.

Now this iron lacework is falling into tatters. The sinuous veins, muscles, nerves are crumbling, slowly, into ash. Deprived of nicotine, the body begins a slow implosion, and so begins the coughing up, spitting out, throwing up.

Throat skinned, raw flesh raked over with a razor blade. I hear a voice speak—harsh, cracked, nasal. As the voice speaks there's a searing pain. I hear it through blocked ears, a blocked heavy aching head. The voice slurs. What in hell's name has it got to do with me, this slurring voice slithering over words, choking? I've never lost my voice before, and even now it's not that I'm losing it. You'd think, the way it's put—"losing your voice"—that I'd been careless and left it behind somewhere. No, it's not that I'm losing it: it's being wrenched from me, brutally.

This is retribution. To renounce and then have to endure punishment, over and above the agony of not-having—it's as though you're being punished for renunciation itself.

You're meant to feel better and it's true at moments—after the manic fixated running or swimming or concentrated visualization of idyllic scenes filled with water and greenery and lithe blond boys, for a moment before the craving invades all sensation, for a moment when you wake half consciously to a fresh mouth before the habitual desire stirs, for a moment . . . No. No, it doesn't happen sequentially like that. Again: you stir enjoying that dreamy drowsy stirring state and along with it comes a nuzzling desire, habitual, familiar. At the same time you feel your mouth—clean, clear. This conscious feeling displaces momentarily the old demands. You "feel" your head —not groggy, not hungover. You feel it's possible to be alert, bright eyed and bushy tailed in the early morning, even good-natured. Perhaps. Then the comfortable and familiar niggle of desire starts gnawing. You want to sleep to block all this out, but you have to get up. So you get up to deal with another day, another prolonged endurance test. It begins again.

So in a perverse way I welcome this ritual of retribution, this so visible breakdown, this coughing aching feverish folly. I embrace the decay—because it *is* visible, so evidently somatic. Otherwise, you exist in the world, move through social space as though "together." But the sensation is of being in pieces—a smashing, splintering, aching. All wanting, needing.

When your voice is wrenched from your throat and you choke on the blood, then you can't say what you want. Evidently.

"Feeling" the mouth, "feeling" the head. Smoking, feelings. Some would ask: what were you not dealing with in smoking, what feelings were you avoiding? They assume that smoking entails false feelings, or at least avoidance, and that renunciation paves the way for a more authentic, less destructive way of experiencing the world. They posit a prelapsarian moment of authenticity—to be recaptured, grasped in the renunciating gesture. All I feel is wretched.

BABIES OR BOOZE

(metonymy)

∽

It's Acland Street on a gray weekday morning. The street is washed out, almost emptied of people, but the cake shops are open and full of cakes. Rows and rows of cakes in brilliant succulent colors line the street. A sweet facade. A few sleepy pedestrians meander across the road, dodging the tram as it rolls around the bend, leaving the ocean and Luna Park, carrying its few passengers back into urban density. I buy a newspaper and amble toward Sheherezade, where the old men drink coffee and talk in Yiddish.

Walking toward me I see a woman with a pram. She glides along the pavement oblivious of other people, who have to swerve and dodge or skip sideways as she approaches. Gazing lovingly into the pram, she seems supremely contented, self-contained; her look is drawn and held by something there, in the interior. I imagine the baby—crinkly eyes, a curious yet gratified smile fidgeting across its face.

I'm overwhelmed by simultaneous identification and envy. I am a mother, gliding, centered absolutely and forever by that enchanting fidgety smile. At the same time I hate her, that smugness—what right has she to this obscene reveling in maternal possession? Why her, not me?

We are drawn together, along a vector that stretches through the space of Acland Street. There is a rattling in the air. We approach, pass in slow-motion. I gaze into the pram.

It is filled with bottles. Rattling bottles dense with amber liquid. Beer bottles.

There it is, in the heart of the perambulator: a substitution. One way or another, it keeps coming back: babies or booze.

BOMBS OR BUMS

(metaphor)

⌒

She dreams, surfing the freeway. Her board: a battered rent-
a-wreck, transformed by the Los Angeles night into a gleaming streamlined machine, one among a million others, gliding
into the future. She feels at last like a local, all her confidence
invested in this native car, all her faith focused on its ability to
take her home. It wasn't always so. She remembers when she
first arrived in L.A. and started driving on the freeways, it felt
as though she were driving against the traffic, driving into a
maelstrom, like the aliens in *Earth Girls Are Easy*. In a car for
the first time, they are propelled backwards at great speed,
plowing through a car wash, totaling a gas station, and zip-
ping in reverse onto the freeway. Once there they manage to
shift gears, only to find themselves racing forward into six
lanes of oncoming traffic. But tonight she feels part of it all.
Cars zip in and out of lanes, lights veer and streak, and over
everything there is a roar, even over the Rolling Stones who
still can't get no satisfaction, and who still can't get it very
loudly, on K-Earth 101. Over everything there is the roar of
the freeway at night.

She dreams and drives. And drives. And drives. Time
passes, and the exit signs flash past, scarcely tickling her pe-
ripheral vision. She starts to pay attention now and realizes
the exits are unfamiliar, somehow, somewhere she and her
rent-a-wreck must have veered off course.

She exits and pulls into the first service station she sees,
parks and digs out her *Thomas Guide*. But where to start? She
has a vague idea that she's been traveling north, off the 101,

deep into the heart of the Valley. But this doesn't look like the Valley—it's bleak, deserted, badly lit. She reminds herself that most public spaces in night time L.A, bar the freeway, are bleak, deserted, badly lit. Looking around, trying to figure out the cross streets, she notices that all the gas-station attendants are black. Then she notices that all the people in the only other car are also black. Across the road there's a diner, filled with black eaters. There isn't a single other white person in sight. So now she really does feel like the aliens in *Earth Girls Are Easy*, like she's landed on another planet, and there's no reason to expect that the people on this other planet are going to see her as anything other than an unwelcome intruder. She also feels a horrible affinity with Cher in *Clueless*, who thinks that Bosnia is in the Middle East and Kuwait in the Valley.

An old man ambles towards her, and says "You lost lady?" She's about to feign confidence, to know where she's going and what she's doing, but there she is, a thin white woman sitting in her tinny little car with the great big *Thomas Guide* spread out on her lap. So instead she nods feebly. "OK," he says, "Tell me where you're coming from and where you're heading." She tells him and he starts to laugh, and then he stops laughing and looks at her. "Girl," he says— and she registers the demotion, a girl now, no longer a lady— "Girl, you took a wrong turn a long time ago."

He starts to give her directions. "Turn left onto this street and keep going until you see McDonald's and then turn right and keep going until you see the signs for the 405. Get onto the 405 going south." He looks at her and chuckles— "that's in the direction of Santa Monica." Simple enough, but she's suspicious, it's altogether too simple. Perhaps for a joke he's sending her deeper into his alien domain. Perhaps she'll be tailed by the sinister red Camaro idling on the other side of the pump, its engine rippling, exhaust spluttering, four feisty young black men looking for something to do on Saturday night. She recites the directions back to him, and then asks how far it is to McDonald's. "Listen girl," he says, "just drive, just drive till you see McDonald's, McDonald's is easy to see, you can't miss McDonald's. You don't have to write a book about it."

Off she goes, suspecting she's been hoodwinked, there is no McDonald's at the end of the yellow brick road, she'll never get home again. Gripping the wheel she scans the horizon. And there it is: a large luminous yellow M. Her hands relax on the wheel and in two flicks of a mule's tail she's back on the freeway heading toward Santa Monica.

On the home run she flips the dial on her radio, seeking soothing classical sounds. But it is wild romantic music that floods the car, the L.A. Philharmonic playing Berlioz. Uncanny to hear this music that she had heard live at the Dorothy Chandler Hall the night before, uncanny to hear it now on the freeway—the identical performance respatialized, privatized, given a new temporality by the car radio. Similarly she finds it uncanny the way the conductor materializes on billboards all over L.A—out there, larger than life, he is simultaneously in here, framed by the car window, drawn into the locus of the car. He and the Marlboro Man, who stretches like a lazy giant over Sunset Boulevard, twirling his lasso, about to throw and watch it snake in slithery circles over this city of neon lights. The gigantic Classical Conductor—in black T-shirt, arm aloft, biceps bared and sinuous—holds between his fingers a magic wand that he is about to twirl, conjuring music out of the asphalt, light out of the puddles. In the concert hall you see only his back, the distance between you is formal and regulated, but in the car you encounter him face to face and as you drive he comes closer and closer. The Marlboro Man is pleasingly anachronistic, an icon of savage nostalgia in this petulantly nonsmoking, pollution-saturated city. He always takes her by surprise, and as he rises into view against the night sky a smoky sensation fills the car, a sense of shared intimacy. And when she sees the conductor through the car window she feels her ordinary old daily body tighten, infused by music, becoming extradaily. As though she is again in the front row of the Dorothy Chandler, sitting directly behind him, watching his muscles work under the sober tuxedo, and every time she is amazed that it can make so much difference to be there, in the presence of such a decided body. Through his mediation the music enters her body in a different way, passes in a circuit through all the playing and listening bodies, charges the connection between her and the man she sits close to, not touching, yet. Now, listening to Berlioz crackle on the freeway this memory infiltrates, she is lassoed by the smoke of the Marlboro Man and the magic of the conductor, and something very public enters into her car, mutates, creates an air of privacy.

Eventually she arrives home, switches the engine off and listens to it chug before subsiding, just like her body, still vibrating from the momentum and tension of the long drive. She is glad to be home.

Albeit a temporary home. Everyone in this apartment complex is an impermanent resident—they come from all over America and from the rest of the world, and have little in common. Yet an almost instantaneous camaraderie is forged by their common strangeness, by their all being fleeting inhabitants of L.A. She arrives to an impromptu party in the courtyard around the pool, to barbecue smells and free-flowing wine. Sinking into a pink banana chair, she is drawn into the atmosphere of conviviality. Among the foreigners cigarettes are exchanged and smoke swirls slowly over the pool, caught in the reflection of lights from up the hill. She'd once said to Luisa, from Pisa, "It must be tough these days, being a smoker in California," and Luisa had tossed her head back and laughed a guttural, smoky laugh, "Not at all, this is how I've met people here, how I've made friends."

There's desultory talk of this and that and then the conversation turns jokingly, as it always and inevitably does these days, to the Clinton affair. "The question is," says someone, "do soiled skirts in the White House constitute a public or private matter?" "The real question," someone else retorts, "is this: what do you get when you cross Monica Lewinsky with Ted Kaczynski, the Unabomber?"

The Italian girls answer in singsong unison: "A dynamite blow job."

The Frenchwoman raises her eyebrows. "Perhaps we should not forget," she cautions, "that Monica was the name of Saint Augustine's mother; and it is really Saint Monica who instigates *The Confessions*."

"I beg to differ," says the German. "It is not Saint Augustine we should remember, it is the king. Recall, if you will, the two bodies of the king."

"Siamese Kings!" exclaims Luisa.

The German looks stern. "We are witnessing here an historic moment, the collapse of a symbolic system," he announces. "Tell me, what is the difference—here and now in America—between the upper body and the lower body? There is no difference! No more. And between the public and the private? No distinction!"

The Europeans, well versed in early history, nod knowingly. The postcolonial subjects look bored. Everyone else looks blank.

Then Maggie, an American, speaks: "I believed in Bill Clinton," she says, "and it hurts, what he's done."

SINCE ARRIVING home and subsiding into her banana chair, she has been silent, musing on McDonald's and the Marlboro Man and Berlioz and the Rolling Stones. Now Maggie's confession of pain lures her into the conversation; she finds her mouth unaccountably opening, and words emerging of their own accord:

"What about the bombs?"

There is silence around the table. The pool is absolutely still.

The melancholic Swede pulls out his dental floss dispenser, gazes longingly at it, and then pockets it again. Everyone wants to floss.

Eventually Maggie speaks: "What bums?" She looks bewildered, as if she might have missed a sexual innuendo that the whole of America, except her, had tuned in to.

"Excuse my accent. Let me say it again—what do you think about America dropping BOMBS in Afghanistan and the Sudan?"

"Well," says Maggie, "if people are going to drop bombs on American embassies, what can they expect?"

"And do we know who these people are?" the man from Pakistan inquires. "How do we know that the people targeted by these cruise missile attacks *are* the same people who bombed the embassies?"

BUT WE all do. We all know this because we have seen a single blurred and fleeting image of Osama bin Laden over and over again, repeated on every television channel, on every news broadcast. This will last a week or so. A form of domestic bombing so that the image—like the one of Bill Clinton publicly embracing Monica Lewinsky—becomes part of our intimate decor, like wallpaper. And like wallpaper it will fade, so that eventually all we will remember of this entire incident is the Arab terrorist bin Laden who once bombed American embassies.

SOMEONE CHIPS in excitedly: "Clearly it was a diversion, a *Wag the Dog* situation, a foreign crisis concocted in order to deflect attention!" A convivial atmosphere is restored, the silent witnesses revive, reenter the fray. Talk flows, argument is cordial, everyone has an opinion or a joke about the uncanny way that life imitates art. An air of intimate geniality eddies around the group, flows out, animating again the flat surface of the pool.

"Hang on," says the Mexican, "weren't the bombs in *Wag the Dog virtual* bombs?"

SHE WATCHES Maggie dab at a few stray tears, slip away unobtrusively, and reappear with a tray of elaborately decorated desserts, crystallized fruits, and petits fours. Maggie blows her nose loudly, declaring an end to it all, an end to hurt and betrayal and bickering—"The night is young, and so are we!" She has an image of Maggie as a multipurpose, smoke-free, environmentally safe American machine, conscientiously incorporating public life, assiduously processing it, turning it into the realm of the intimate. She, on the other hand, feels as though she is again driving on the freeway for the first time, propelled into six lanes of oncoming traffic. She recalls that although Geena Davis, Valley Girl supreme, understands that Jeff Goldblum is an alien, she persists in calling his planet by a vaguely familiar name that nevertheless signifies outer space: "Zimbabwe."

Virtual and actual, bombs and bums, public and private, foreign and domestic, inside and outside, smoking and not-smoking. There is a necessity for distinctions, she sees this, but how to negotiate the connections, how to avoid a total occlusion of difference?

Not long ago all she wanted was to get home, but now that she is here she wants only to be safely cocooned in her Rent-a-Wreck, barreling along the 405 with Berlioz and the smoky tracings of the Marlboro Man's lasso. She wonders: do aliens from outer space smoke? And, if so, what? How do they name what they smoke? And do they distinguish between the smoke from cigarettes and the smoke from bombs?

TRACED BY

(A S L I G H T S E N S E O F)

BITTERNESS

∞

Tobacco comes in various guises. It comes loosely packed in tins and in shiny midnight blue plastic pouches and in packages of gold and silver paper. It might be shaggy and rich, a deep mahogany hue, or you might find it falls in amber filaments and smells like honey. It could be sticky to the touch, or dry and flaky. You might first have encountered tobacco in the form of ready-made cigarettes, boxed or packaged, in tens or twenties or thirties. Sometimes it comes and is gone in a puff—a single puff from a single cigarette bought and shared among a group. It comes on occasion in the form of snuff—in beautiful small boxes, inlaid with mother-of-pearl. Or it is to be found in pipes, all kinds of pipes, ranging from short-stemmed, stubby pipes used by sailors for stabbing the air and storytelling, to elaborate underground pipes that enable a group of smokers to lie full length on the ground and to smoke unencumbered by any apparatus. Once upon a time in a distant land, it came in the deliciously arcane form of huge dirty brown balls.

AN AFRICAN MAN squats on the ground in front of an open dome-shaped hut. He is rolling and patting into shape a large, lumpy ball about a foot in diameter. A number of these balls, which look like large constipated elephant turds, are spread around him.

I COME ACROSS this mysterious image in the archives in Harare. It is an old black-and-white photograph, undated, but the caption says: "Making *nyoka* tobacco." Following the word *nyoka*, I discover that this was a traditional way of preparing tobacco employed by the Shangwe people, who lived in an inhospitable area (in the present-day Gokwe district of Zimbabwe) plagued by malaria and sleeping sickness. Nevertheless, in a territory where tobacco was universally cultivated by Africans prior to colonization, the Inyoka country was famous for its tobacco culture and manufacture. After the leaf was picked, it was hung and air cured, then mixed with the ashes of aloes and pounded in mortars. It was dampened with water, then molded into loaves, balls, or cones (weighing on average about three pounds) and placed on platforms to dry. Then, tied on to reed trays, it was ready for transportation. When wanted, the cones were broken into pieces and allowed to dry out, before the very strong and pungent product was smoked in pipes or ground into snuff.

> In Rhodesia we have all the factors making for the building up of a great industry. The sand veld, which comprises so much of the country, is well adapted to tobacco, and is among the cheapest land in the world; the climate, with a short, wet summer and dry weather after the cropping, is such that much of the tobacco can be cured in the open. Labour is fairly plentiful, and, if not as efficient as could be desired, is very low-priced. —"DEVELOPMENT OF THE RHODESIA TOBACCO INDUSTRY," *African World*, 1913

In 1890 a mercenary army recruited by Cecil Rhodes' British South Africa Company invaded Mashonaland and three years later, Matabeleland. Boundaries were redrawn, a new country was created, a country called—after the architect of invasion—Rhodesia. By Christmas 1891 the first white farms had been occupied (allocated by Rhodes for a nominal rent of one pound per year), and in 1895 the first tobacco crop was grown (by Lionel Cripps, a member of the so-called "pioneer column"). And this is how it all began, or so many stories tell us: it was from these farms that the prosperity of Rhodesia would develop, a prosperity based not on gold mined from belowground as had been anticipated but from a weed transformed into a golden leaf, a weed of the Nicotiana family cultivated in gray and sandy soil, nurtured, harvested, traded, exported.

IT SEEMS AS though the discovery of Rhodesia entailed simultaneously the discovery of tobacco, inexpensive land, and plentiful cheap labor. But tobacco was not brought to southern Africa by the "pioneers"; it had been around for a long time before them, probably having been brought by the Portuguese and cultivated since the seventeenth century. Most pre–twentieth century reports come from travelers, hunters, and adventurers, who record smoking habits and the addiction of the indigenous population but do not pay much attention to methods of cultivation, production, and trade. If the natives were smoking like chimneys, where did the tobacco come from? How, I wonder, did tobacco emerge and circulate prior to this golden age of cheap land and a plentiful low-priced labor supply? And could there be any connection between this nirvana (ready-found land, labor, and nicotine) and the fact that we know so little about tobacco production prior to colonization?

A picture is summoned up (in early adventurers' tales) of rather inefficient and hedonistic peasant pastoralists—addicts cultivating a few plants here and there in a haphazard fashion, just as hippies supposedly grow dope and share it out, squandering it among friends. And then with the transition to a new economy, the inefficient peasants are transformed into inefficient labor. In this scenario the peasants, not sophisticated enough to compete with the efficiency of capitalist methods and unable to support themselves by agriculture, become dependent for survival upon wages earned in "white" industrial regions or on white farms.

In fact, of course, indigenous populations in every colonized country, utilizing local knowledges, invented forms of resistance to and independence from wage employment. And in part they were able to exercise these forms of resistance because the capitalist machinery was less efficient than often supposed in the history books. During the early period of colonial rule in Rhodesia, there was comparative prosperity in the reserves as traditional subsistence methods were adapted for a new situation: the production of cash crops. This self-sufficiency and avoidance of wage labor posed an obstacle for the colonial rulers, who had to exert extra efforts to undermine the viability of the peasant sector. Their main way of responding was through the imposition of taxes: hut tax, poll tax, dog tax, rents, dipping fees, and so on. Peasants, in their turn, attempted to meet the demands of colonial governments for tax by seeking to earn money their own way.

Tobacco—in particular the cultivation of *nyoka* tobacco by the Shangwe—was one of the avenues of evasion and independence.

In the precolonial era when the area was dominated by the Ndebele, the Shangwe paid dues in the form of tobacco to Lobengula, king of Matabeleland. The Ndebele themselves grew large quantities of tobacco both for pipes and snuff, which they took on all social occasions and usually carried with them in horn containers. However, it seems that despite their own large supply, the Ndebele prized the Inyoka variety of tobacco as unique and definitely superior. Because of this demand the Shangwe were able to offset the dues they were forced to pay by also trading tobacco. A similar situation developed under the colonists—because of the income generated by the tobacco trade, the Shangwe were able to pay the native taxes and resist going to work as labor on white farms. Initially the European occupation aided the Inyoka trade, increasing the market on the periphery of Matabeleland as farms and mines were established. Tobacco was now easier to sell because money was available, whereas before the Shangwe presumably relied on a barter system (since nothing much would grow in the Inyoka country besides tobacco, they probably bartered for grain and other subsistence items).

By 1903 European traders were coming to the area to buy *nyoka* tobacco, and white farmers tried to move in and appropriate this successful enterprise. During 1906 the Inyoka Rhodesia Tobacco Company was formed in London, with Frank Johnson of Pioneer Column fame as its chairman. It was a total failure and became insolvent in 1914.

The years of prosperity continued until 1922. In 1918 the chiefs gave generously to War Fund contributions, Chireya (the paramount chief, or *Inyoka*) providing:

30 cakes of Inyoka tobacco
£3/18/6
21 native made mats

Eventually, however, a number of factors conspired to defeat the Shangwe and eradicate (by the late 1950s) their tobacco production. The 1932 crop was the last that managed to meet the Shangwe tax bill. During drought and famine they received no government support or subsidies and were unable to compete with the developing white industry in terms of dealing with crop diseases (probably exacerbated by overproduction in the 1920s) or to benefit from the European research station established in 1924. One of the main reasons for the decline of the industry is the penetration of the African market by flue-cured Virginia tobacco sold as cigarettes. A Salisbury firm, targeting the younger generation, began to produce cigarettes at ten for a penny, in brightly colored packs with a crocodile or lion on the wrapping.

By the late 1950s the dark and pungent Inyoka tobacco existed no longer, or only as a sensory memory trace for those lucky or unlucky enough to have lived before the advent of the cigarette. In a certain form, however, it still exists: in a crumpled black-and-white photo preserved in the archives. When I first came upon this photo, those strange lumpy elephant turds seemed totally mysterious, bearing no imaginable relation to tobacco as we know it, to the culture of tobacco as manifested predominantly in cigarette smoking. For those who lived before the advent of the cigarette, I had only pity (for the pleasures they were unwittingly denied) or envy (for the tortures they were spared). They seemed, moreover, these strange lumps, to bear no relation to tobacco at all, certainly not to bear in any way upon the insistently metonymic connection between this country (be it Zimbabwe or Rhodesia) and tobacco. But as I have burrowed away in the archives, reading all sorts of records, I have also returned constantly to this photograph as a signpost, a center of gravity; and gradually it has begun to emanate a smell, to change its texture. As I pick it up and run my fingers over its surface, the large lumps start to crumble and a pungency wafts up and fills the archive. "This country" decomposes; its borders and internal divisions are realigned. It becomes, at the very least, more than one country: it becomes Matabeleland and Mashonaland. Present-day Gokwe fades into the past, usurped by the Inyoka country, the tobacco fields and barns and auction rooms where I grew up are replaced by an open dome-shaped hut where a dark tobacco leaf is air cured. Here in the archives a different history of tobacco in this country starts working its way into my being, insinuating different memories, so that oddly enough cigarettes now seem to me rather arcane.

Now I am more intrigued and lured by that pungent odor, traced by a slight bitterness: a scarcely incipient memory of tobacco leaf pounded in a mortar with the ashes of aloes.

INSTEAD OF A LOBOTOMY

(a cigarette)

⌒

Instead of giving her a lobotomy he gives her a cigarette. She is instantly cured. Through this exchange, he is redeemed as the good doctor and she is transformed from a raving loon into a perfect lamb.

"He" is Montgomery Clift and "she" is Elizabeth Taylor, and this scenario transpires in *Suddenly, Last Summer*. It opens like a horror movie: in an insane asylum where zombified, vacant, violent women taunt and are taunted by their keepers, a gang of sadistic nuns. Ominously one of the women is led away, and the next thing we see is a woman unconscious in an operating theater. Before our very eyes Monty performs a lobotomy. It's touch-and-go, the doctor is sweating, the conditions are primitive. Against all odds he performs the miraculous surgery but threatens afterward to withdraw his services unless he is better supported. Lo and behold a patroness appears, in the person of Katharine Hepburn.

In return for her patronage she requests a favor: if she makes it possible for Dr. Monty to perform lobotomies, then he must reciprocate by exercising his surgical skill upon her mad niece, Liz Taylor. In his first meeting with Liz in the madhouse, Dr. Monty senses a connection between her frenzy and the nuns' ban on smoking. So he offers her a cigarette and she is immediately transformed; when the nuns, as is their wont, prepare to restrain her in a straitjacket, she shows no signs of resistance, demonstrating through her demeanor that restraint is unnecessary, and she delivers one of the great movie lines: "Since I was allowed to smoke, I've become a perfect lamb."

Dramaturgically speaking this is a good thing, because it enables Hepburn to take center stage, to monopolize the madness quotient. Always an actress with a fine propensity for histrionic nuance, in this role she surpasses herself, propelled way over the top in a series of hothouse monologues. These monologues are most peculiarly modulated: the way she breathes, the way she runs her sentences together, the way she throws her gaze fixedly off center—all of this is truly weird and yet compelling. We, like the good doctor, suspect that she is telling stories, and we realize that she is out to frame the innocent Liz (who is no match for her when it comes to storytelling and, besides, has lost her memory). But why? we ask. What is the secret so dire that it demands human sacrifice? And why is Liz the victim?

Dr. Monty is no ordinary doctor, he is a mind man, and he knows that there is a way out: if the lobotomy ensures forgetfulness then the truth drug provides an avenue for remembering. He is also a surgeon, blessed with theatrical flair, and so he prepares to inject Liz with the truth drug, setting the scene, ensuring an audience. Under the influence of this drug her repressed memories erupt, and she burbles forth, narrating a tale of horror. It is a story of the sea and of sea creatures, a gruesome parable of carnage, ghosted by a domestic incest scenario. It is hypnotic, and utterly cinematic, an instantiation of the Aristotelian mode cinematized—of narrating rather than showing. It surpasses Marlon Brando doing the "horror, the horror," recalling rather Orson Welles, in *The Lady from Shanghai*, when he tells the tale of the sharks that consume one another, turning the sea red.

Now there's a question posed by this movie, a question pertaining both to the ontology and to the cultural capital (or call it narrative potential?) of the cigarette. The question—posed implicitly, even perhaps unknowingly—is this: is the gift of a cigarette akin to a drug, a healing substance? Or, is it nicotine deprivation that drove Liz mad in the first place? If the former, then we can trace a metonymic chain through the movie, a chain of associations that is distinct from the main narrative but that blows through it, smoking it out, as it were. In this schema the first gift, the curative cigarette, paves the way for the second gift, the truth drug, which in its turn provides the conditions of possibility for revelation and resolution. If, on the other hand, the answer consists in the latter alternative, then the gift of the drug constitutes merely a restoration, a reassertion of the status quo, a return (from madness) to normal neurosis and constitutive unhappiness.

In fact the distinction between these two choices is not so clear-cut. It is the lobotomy that would provide a definitive cut, ensuring forgetfulness; the choice of a cigarette, over a lobotomy, ensures memory. As to the question of whether the cigarette is curative (and transformative) or restorative (and conservative), the movie gives us not so much an answer as a circuitry in which horror, storytelling, and cigarette smoking are intricately enmeshed.

Perhaps they always are. What *Suddenly, Last Summer* does is throw the connections into sharp relief.

Most horror movies are propelled by a singular question: why is this happening, why the madness and the horror, oh the horror? The best answer is given by *Wes Craven's New Nightmare:* this is what happens when stories die. Yet paradoxically, the horror unleashed when people allow stories to die (when they forget) can only be apprehended through a form of storytelling, through the horror movie itself. Just like the cigarette. When you give up smoking (involuntarily like Liz Taylor, or voluntarily—I suppose—like me) stories die: you go mad or you can no longer write, you are bereft of memories transformable into stories. Yet paradoxically, when you give up smoking all you can do is tell horror stories—tell stories, that is, of the horror induced by nicotine deprivation.

If *Suddenly, Last Summer* throws into sharp relief the intricate connections between horror, storytelling, and cigarette smoking, it might also register (and is able to do so by virtue of being generically indeterminate, on the borderline of horror) something more general about the connection between smoking and the movies. In *Suddenly, Last Summer* there is no concept of the unconscious and no such thing as involuntary memory. The cigarette precedes the truth drug, and in this metonymic chain is primarily a device. Ultimately, though, it is not the cigarette itself that is vital to the circuitry but something less tangible, more persistent and pervasive. It is the smoke that matters, it is the smoke that swirls like the unconscious, that sets the scene for storytelling, that lingers as an afterimage. As when Orson Welles uses his cigarettes to seduce, blows smoke out over the world of the film as a prelude to his story of the sharks. He tells his story without the aid of a cigarette, but smoke from earlier in the film lingers, filtering the words and images.

TO REMEMBER

(to find yourself in fragments)

⌒

The music fades away and only then, in the moment of fading, is she aware of the music. And the footsteps.

A man crouches in the stairwell, submerged in shadow. Menace lurks on the edge of the frame. In the silent hours of the early morning footsteps grow closer. She holds her breath.

A burst of pain. Her gaze is wrenched from the screen, flashes over this room where she eats and writes and watches television. Now there's a smell of charred embers and cigarette butts and freesias, the scent seeping into her body, a sweet insinuating nausea. She wraps herself around in an old red blanket, the cat purrs on, the pain momentarily subsides.

Now he's in an office, or is it an office? The room is evenly lit, discreetly opulent. What happened to the footsteps? He refuses the couch, paces the room. Now that he's out of the shadows, you can see who he is. He's Gregory Peck. The other man is short and bald. He asks a lot of questions.

What is the last thing you can remember?
What do you do for a living?
You don't seem like a cost accountant.
Why does that remark agitate you?
Close your eyes and try to remember.

SHE CLOSES her eyes and remembers.

I'd like you to leave immediately. You're a con man and you're in trouble and I don't want any part of it.

What are you talking about? Of course I'm in trouble [says Gregory Peck], that's why I'm here. I need your help. I can't remember. I can't even remember who I am, for Christ's sake.

Clinically, the amnesia you describe doesn't exist. Your story might work on people who want to hear stories, but I'm an analyst, not a detective. I suggest you leave now, this instant—go and find yourself a hired gun.

Gregory Peck stands his ground, a man of marble. Only his facial muscles move. Abruptly he strides across the room and pauses in the doorway. Cut to a close up as he turns and speaks:

You might be a fine scientist, but you're a lousy doctor.

The door slams. The sound reverberates as his footsteps fade. She feels the impact of the door slamming. She wants an ending now, to know how it will end although she knows how it will end: in loss and relief and memories.

He's running now, running for his life in the streets of New York. You can hear his breathing but not his footsteps. A gunshot rings out and he falls to the ground. Silence. Everything freezes. Then he jumps up, runs for cover, crouching under a bridge on the edge of a park. You see, from his point of view, two men across the park talking under a tree. The image is held a fraction too long, too intense a scrutiny. For there is little to see: just two men in a park, in extreme long shot. The image wavers, on the verge of dissolving, and then the camera begins a slow zoom in. The two men grow larger, filling the contours of the frame, and suddenly you are hit: a shock of recognition. One of the men is yourself: Gregory Peck.

She closes her eyes and images immediately appear on her retina, familiar images from a childhood dream. She sees a monochrome landscape: long grass moving in the wind, an avenue of trees winding from a dirt road through an immensity of space to a farmhouse. Slowly, almost imperceptibly, color seeps into the image. Brown grass, the grass of Africa, dry, weighted with dust. She is a little girl, perhaps six or seven, standing in front of the farmhouse, looking directly down the avenue of trees. She feels the earth shudder. In the distance she sees a moving mass of bodies. They march slowly but inexorably closer. Their feet tramping, they are swinging pangas. Closer and closer.

The pains are coming closer and closer.

Gregory Peck is in a detective's office. It is night. The venetian blinds cast diagonal shadows across the room, slicing his body into segments. He says, "I've remembered something." But it is too late. The detective's been murdered. Again, he is alone.

AND WHERE the hell are you? What use is an old red blanket, or a dead detective, when it's you I want? And if you are not here, then I want no witnesses to this sordid and solitary exhibition, I want only obliteration. I will serve myself up on a platter, a writ of erasure: an empty plate, a blank screen, no salves to curiosity or grief.

ACROSS A PARK two figures. Figures in a landscape. A slow fade to black. And back again. The image repeats convulsively. Dissolves. A mirage. Suddenly he is looking down the barrel of a gun.

She looks down the avenue of trees. Can smell the jacaranda blooms falling, crushed underfoot. She turns and runs, into the house, this house where her body has always been cradled. Now there is no hiding place, no escape from the shuddering. She grabs her red blanket flung down amid cats dozing on the veranda, she hugs it to her and runs into the kitchen. There the woodstove burns and embers never die and Moses stirs the stew day after day. He says, "I will hide you." He leads her to the washing basket, large and woven in cane, pink paint peeling. Pulling out some dirty clothes, he makes a nest. Lifting her in his arms, he places her in the basket, wraps the blanket around her, and says, "You must be quiet as a mouse and hold your breath." Then he puts the lid over her head.

She is glad to be invisible, to be as small as a mouse. She is not at all surprised that Moses has magic—she has always known, secretly, that he is a *n'anga*. But there is something that surprises, that eludes her grasp.

Nestled in her blanket, she feels a stab of nausea. Her body registers a premonition, conceives a memory—of guilt and treachery—that will return, too late.

The footsteps recur. *Tramp, tramp, tramp.* The sound grows closer; it fills the frame of the house. Doors slam; she feels the impact of a steel blade slashing into glass. Through the slats of the washing basket she sees the laundry window splinter, a cascade of green glass light streaming into the room. In the shaft of light that falls through the smashed window, that falls across the room to the edge of her basket, she sees feet approaching. She holds her breath, enduring the menace of suffocation. If she can see so clearly, surely they can see her for what she is: a white girl waiting. But the feet pass by, clamoring, searching.

By watching intently she finds she can see everything. Through that minute space between slats, the world is opened up like a map. Once she looked through her father's camera and was enchanted. But this is better.

She sees the backyard, the chopping block where the chickens have their heads chopped off and run around bleeding, frenzied. There are no chickens now, no people. The frame is empty, waiting for something to take place.

Then they enter, a multitude of bodies, men and women with bright bandannas wound around their heads and babies on their backs, wrapped around with blankets. The air vibrates with the sound of their shouting, the grinding, as pangas are sharpened. Then a space clears around the chopping block, the sound fades. In the moment of its fading, she knows what will happen, knows that if she looks now she will never see again. But she cannot not watch.

She watches as her mother and father are led into the clearing. One at a time they are made to kneel by the block, the back of their necks bared. Then a panga, a single panga, is raised. Suddenly, unwaveringly, it plummets—ripping in a flash through air and flesh.

A convulsion, a last gasp for air pulls her out of the childhood dream and into the present. She feels it slip: smoothly like a slip of the tongue it slides from her body. Between her legs it lies: this clot, vaguely familiar.

She lifts her eyes to the television. The movie is over, there are only ads for take-away foods, the colors too bright, the sentiments too intense, the sounds too harsh. She will never know how it ended: whether he found his memory, why it mattered so much, why Walter Matthau died.

THE SKY lightens. You come. You wrap your arms around me and I feel your breath on the back of my neck, your hand on my face, and I know my body is not in pieces.

IN THE HOSPITAL she lies on her back and watches the screen. The ultrasound black-and-white image is mesmerizing: dense and abstract. There is movement, resistance and flow. She can almost grasp the contours of the image and then they slither, disperse, reshape. In the background voices murmur of sound waves. Straining to look, she sees there in the screen a delineation: two figures in a landscape. A slow zoom begins and she recoils.

The doctor speaks: "You can relax now. It's all over, clever girl—you got rid of it all by yourself. You can go home and forget."

Reprieved, she lights up a cigarette and feels suddenly light headed, euphoric, as though smoking for the very first time. They rush to find food, ravenous, desirous of tasting for the first time textures of the unknown. They laugh and tell each other stories. "Has the pain gone, really gone?" he asks. She tells him that already it is like a nightmare that in its dreaming has left an imprint, obscure, but no more troubling than an acne scar. "Was it better this way," he asks, "to know it in the body, or would it be better to be unconscious, to never know?" She sees the anxiety around his eyes and knows that he knows there is no answer. She cannot tell him what it is to be in a woman's body, for she does not know, in spite of everything, she does not know.

Hearing foreign voices, she turns and her gaze sweeps over the restaurant, out through the window, opening onto a scene from the past. She sees a small girl crouched in the sunlight by a group of men sitting outside a tobacco barn. Her father is there, and some black men. They laugh and argue and exchange cigarettes. She looks past them out across a field of maize, deep green in the burnt red soil. She imagines the succulence of young mealies, cooked over embers, smoky. She dreams to the cadenced rhythm of Shona speech. Suddenly a voice speaks in English, a Shona voice speaking to her father in his own tongue: "But remember, come the Long Night and we'll be on different sides of the fence."

A barbed-wire fence, strewn, entangled over an immense space.

Is this what it is to remember, she thinks: to dismember, to find yourself in fragments. Across the table he is speaking, telling her a tale of intrigue and mystery. She forgets everything else and only wants to know what happens next.

To forget, she traveled, and she was a good traveler. She'd traversed the globe, never looking back, never yearning to return. Now, out of the blue, she starts remembering.

She is enjoying fresh sardines and black olives with lemon wedges and chunks of thick crusty bread, all served up on a terra-cotta plate. Perched on a low wall, looking down on the Mediterranean Sea, she crunches the last of the bones, uses the last chunk of bread to mop up the oil, and then holds her plate up against the sky. Terra-cotta against blue. Cats are gathering around her—scraggy, shy, and vicious cats, feral and feisty, tabby and ginger and black-and-white. They mewl and growl at one another and bare their fangs at her. They are waiting for her to toss them her fish bones, but she has eaten everything. She spits back at them: "Tonight you eat mice."

She remembers, from a childhood poem, the dormouse who simply wanted to be left alone to sleep in a bed "of delphiniums blue and geraniums red." As a child she was captivated by the exoticism of these words, the sensation they evoked of saturated color, the surprise of their syllabic unfolding.

She too would like to bury her head in the blue sand.

She unzips her shoulder bag and rummages, reaching inside for a hidden waterproof pocket that contains a casually sacred object, her travel charm. It is a black-and-white photograph clipped to a rather crumpled, flattened-out blue pack. The black-and-white photograph is of a fat black-and-white cat; the pack is a Gitanes pack. She had forgotten they even existed, but now suddenly remembering she feels touched, brushed by the wings of an angel. Albeit a tarnished angel. In the beginning there had been only the Gitanes charm, and as she'd put it in her bag when starting out on her travels, she'd thought to herself: not so much a Saint Christopher, more like Saint Jude—the saint of lost causes.

In the beginning—at the start of her round-the-world journey, that is—there had been a renunciation. She had given up smoking. She smoked her last Gitanes in the departure lounge, and as her flight was called, she stubbed out the cigarette she was smoking and scrunched up the pack, about to throw it into the garbage. But then the blueness of it arrested the gesture, she had a sudden craving to curl up in delphiniums blue and geraniums red. Instead she emptied out the remaining cigarettes, watched them fall one by one into the garbage; she smoothed out the pack and contemplated the gypsy girl, the swirl, the sense of adventure: "Hey Jude . . . take a sad song and make it better."

It had been surprisingly easy, giving up, an act simple to perform and without entailment. She got on the airplane and started flying, into the blue, into the future. From then on everything seemed to happen at the speed of light. For the first time in years she could taste the food she ate and even airplane food tasted divine, looked enticing—a sophisticated version of the TV dinners they used to eat while watching *Rawhide*. Where it used to be cold chops, deliciously greasy, that you could eat with your fingers, now it was braised cutlets with baby carrots and potato croquettes; where it was once crystallized cherries, it was now cherry tomatoes. The reassuring continuity continued in the person of Clint himself, still there on a small screen, a bit more gravel in the voice, a few more scars and wrinkles. After finishing his chop and before moving on to the little tub of emerald green jelly, their father would light up a Peter Stuyvesant and use his dinner tray as an ashtray, ash and food mingling, and then he would continue eating, and through it all he would be watching. These activities—eating, smoking, Clint—all segued messily into one another. Clint was an activity, he happened once a week, and you "did" him: smoked him, ate him, and somehow secured his continuance long after he rode off, out of the living room and into the wilderness "through rain and wind and weather." It was a form of cannibalism and an act of transubstantiation. So now he returns, rides in out of the rain and wind and weather, out of *The Unforgiven*, to hail her in this capsule in the sky: "Hey you (eating) remember me (being eaten), make my day!" Of course she remembers, but in this moment she also forgets. As she looks away from Clint, looks down at her plastic container scraped clean of food—no ash, no cigarette stubs—she begins to forget: her father, Clint, the taste of cigarettes.

After this she doesn't think about the past, about the taste of cigarettes, about redundant heroes. She is avid for new adventures, unrecognizable desires, strange bedfellows. And miraculously this is what she finds. When she steps off the plane at JFK, she meets a man and falls in love. The first three months she is deliriously happy. Then for the next three months she is deliriously unhappy. And then her lover is gone and she is simply wretched. Her mind goes blank, her body aches, every bone feels brittle, and her flesh flounders. Colliding with foreign bodies she bruises, experiences herself as untouchable, black and blue all over. She stops eating and avoids contact with the world. At first, when the phone rings she says, "I'm fine. And you?" but after a while she just lets it ring. Unable to concentrate on reading, she watches television; at first her attention spans the duration of an ad, but slowly she becomes more competent and is able to watch the television reruns channel. The shows all blend into one another, just like the cigarettes and food and Clint. Then, all of a sudden during an old episode of *The Mary Tyler Moore Show* things change: there is a moment that stands out, isolatable as a moment. Rhoda has been mourning the end of a relationship and tells Mary how she was watching TV and how sad it was when John Boy died. Mary says, "He didn't die. He's the star of the show." "Well," says Rhoda, "something died tonight. It was there in the TV."

The next day she picked up the phone, a foreign object that this time didn't bruise, and dialed her friend Maggie. "He left me," she wailed, "and he left nothing behind, no mementos, no photos, no nothing. He's fading fast, and I'm so scared that soon he'll be gone completely and I'll be all alone forever, and it's no wonder—I'm so awful, so untouchable, and I'm homesick, and Nekko's dead, and I want to smoke." "Give us a break," said Maggie. "You aren't the only one." "But you aren't alone," she said. "You've got Viola." "Big deal," said Maggie, "like it's all I ever wanted, to go to my grave being loved by a cat. An ugly cat moreover."

Maggie had taken her to eat at Mario's, anachronistic in its aspirations to *Godfather* splendor, its opulence old-fashioned and faded. The moment you walked in, you began to feel like a gangster's moll, or even a gangster, and you began to feel hungry. They were seated at a table next to painted plaster cherubs supporting dusty glass candelabra. Maggie ordered red wine and ossobuco for both of them, and while they were waiting opened her purse and spilled the contents—driver's license, credit cards, lipstick, insurance cards, a few photographs, some tampons—onto the table. She rifled through till she found what she was looking for—a photograph of Viola—and presented it to her friend as a gift: a small rather crumpled black-and-white photograph of a fat black-and-white cat.

On the wall opposite them there was an almost trompe l'oeil mural. It seemed as though the red velvet carpet (faded now but exuding an eternal air of shabby grandeur) rolled out of the restaurant into a garden of unearthly delights: vines drooping under the weight of purple fruit, a pond shrouded by gauzy green fronds through which you could just make out the luscious shapes of almost-naked Titian-type women. Though if you looked closely, you could see vestiges of black-and-white geometrical bathing costumes and Carnaby Street towels: maidens from another era, another palimpsest, brought to life by persistence of vision. They drank red wine and told intricate stories of family feuds and hired guns and paltry obsessions. As the evening wore on, their stories became more rhetorically ornate, each one more elegantly gruesome than the last, more and more marvelous.

Back home she looked closely at Maggie's photograph, at this precious object turned so casually into a gift. She looked at Viola, a fat black-and-white cat she had never met, and she began to weep. She wept and wept, not for Viola but for her own cat, Nekko, who had sat on her desk for ten years, purring when the computer was turned on, spitting when 108 asked to move off the delphinium blue thesaurus, glowering through the cigarette smoke. Then she had finished her book, stopped smoking, and Nekko died—killed in the night by a dog. Maggie had realized more than she had: that it was for her cat and her years of writing and smoking that she mourned, not for the man she'd known for six months. Or to put it differently: she had been missing him, acutely even, but mainly because he stood in for other things. It wasn't his fault the way things had turned out—she sees now that she had asked of him the impossible, to be something he wasn't.

A man is no substitute for a cigarette. A photograph is no substitute for a thing. One cat cannot replace another. All this she realized, looking at the photo, but she also apprehended its importance for the future. She would keep it close, together with her blue Gitanes pack, as a travel charm and as a mnemonic. She would keep it to remember Maggie, and the man as well, but also because it marked the moment when she began to forget him. She would keep it for other reasons too, for even though it might be true that a photograph is no substitute for a thing, and so on and so on, it is only through a serial meandering of substitutions and transformations that we survive desire, that desire survives.

Now back in the present, as she finishes her sardines and picks up a pen rather than a cigarette, she thinks of Kafka, who wrote: "We photograph things in order to drive them out of our minds. My stories are a way of shutting my eyes."

CHAOS

Out of control, chaotic, turbulent: this is how the addict is often characterized. Yet smoking, or sniffing, or needling (that is, the practice of feeding a needing, not the needing per se) imposes an order—if only the order of continuity, of linearity, the assurance of one thing leading to another, to the same, to a repetition. It is only with withdrawal that this chaos and turbulence are unleashed.

Yet if every passion, as Benjamin remarks, borders on the chaotic, cigarette smoke surely evinces the waviness of the border. As a phenomenon it is often cited as one of the simplest examples of chaos—the smoke rises in a spiral from the cigarette, then suddenly it breaks up; its trajectory becomes chaotic, random. This moment, when laminar or smooth flow dissolves into nonlaminar flow, can't be predicted or determined, and neither can the pattern of dispersal be foretold.

SMOKO

∽

Onstage the soldiers loll around, lazily exchanging jokes, polishing their sabers, playing cards. And then the gates of the cigarette factory open and out come the girls. They sashay into the square, look the men up and down, light up. It is a moment of transition, that moment before the drama begins: a liminal zone of somnolence is charged, the men become instantly alert to every move the women make. And the women make their moves slowly. At first they are almost indifferent to the men, relishing instead their independence, taking time to taste the taste of freedom, to taste tobacco. They blow smoke rings, which rise and circle over the stage, entangling and taunting the soldiers, who sing:

> *Look at them! Their insolent stares,*
> *their flirtatious looks!*
> *Each one with a cigarette*
> *between her lips!*

From the audience she looks back, sees the smoke signals, senses the danger that is about to unfurl as *Carmen* begins. In the very moment that she senses danger, her body also registers a taste of freedom.

Radford, Nottingham, 1968: she is sixteen years old, has just left home, taken her first job, and experienced—for the first time in her life—a sense of independence. When she began working in the Players Cigarette factory, a whole new world opened up a self-contained world, a world wreathed in smoke rings. She lived, along with all the other employees, in Players Village—an elaborate complex that included housing, and amenities, and the cigarette factory. Every day she gave thanks for her escape from poverty, from a crowded house, from the smell of stewed brussels sprouts, now replaced by nicotine fumes. Here, like the other women, she earned £12 a week. This was a lot of money (even though it was exactly half of what the men earned), and there were perks in addition to these wages: everyone who worked there was given a certain number of free cigarettes—women got thirty a week and men, sixty. Moreover, a blind eye was turned to stealing cigarettes off the conveyor belt, though only during breaks. So it seemed to her at first, gifts—in this kingdom of plenty—proliferated.

Leaving home she discovered the world, and the world was Players Village. Rising at 4 A.M. each morning and working Saturdays, work and leisure segued into each other, just as the smoko—the time it takes to smoke a cigarette—both punctured and punctuated work time, proffering at once a radical reprieve and a reassuring continuity. Everyone was allowed one toilet break a session, and smokers were also allowed a smoking break. At first she didn't smoke, and basked in the beneficence of giving away as gifts her quota of cigarettes, but once she realized she was missing out on "free time" she too, like all the others before her, became a smoker and got a second break by joining the smoko.

When she first started work, she was assigned to making Players No. 6, and one of her tasks was floor sweeping. Since No. 6 was a cheap cigarette, made up mainly of debris that littered the factory floor, she spent a good deal of her time sweeping. Later she was promoted to making Grosvenors, a posh cigarette, and then she felt like Cinderella at the ball—no more sweeping. Here she was assigned the job of packing the cigarettes into boxes, a task that required much dexterity and a finely tuned sense of timing and rhythm. You would lift one cigarette in each hand and simultaneously lower them into the boxes whizzing around on the conveyor belt. The most exciting thing you could do was called "stop the line"—

this involved jamming up the works by, for instance, not putting both hands down at once. Cigarettes would fly in all directions, alarms would sound, the conveyor belt would shudder to a halt, supervisors would rant and rave, but through everyone else, through all the workers, would pass something akin to an electric current of camaraderie. It was during union disputes that she learned to "stop the line," to use the elements that constituted her dependence (as she now realized) as a mode of resistance.

All the unskilled jobs in the factory were allocated to women, and there were few avenues of escape; eventually she came to experience it as an exploitative and addictive industry. But this is also where she experienced, for the first time, a sense of her own potential power and simultaneously a sense of connection to a world more extensive and liberating than she had imagined or encountered. The Tobacco Workers Union was militant and exciting; for a sixteen-year-old girl it provided an entrée to an operatic world characterized by a passionate orchestration of quotidian politics. In this world of agonistic theatricalization, she learned to play different roles and eventually to maneuver her way out of the factory. In the process of becoming dependent on nicotine, she also acquired independence: most obviously, in earning her own money, she acquired a degree of economic autonomy; less obviously, her imbrication in the world of cigarettes enabled a degree of sexual autonomy. Working on the assembly line, packing cigarettes, she was unequal; but like Carmen, the defiant gypsy girl, she discovered that there was a way to be the equal of men—through *smoking* cigarettes. And if the factory owners used the smoko to measure and to designate industrial time, she learned from her women friends and coworkers how to stretch the smoko. Through smoking she learned how to stretch time, to slow things down, to languorously unravel desire. She discovered that she could inhale and hold the smoke and breathe it out slowly, and just as she might move her tongue languidly or teasingly over a cigarette in her mouth, so she might move her tongue when entangled with another body. She came to understand, through somatic rather than cognitive means, that she too could choose, could pleasure and be pleasured.

Look at them! Their insolent stares,
their flirtatious looks!
Each one with a cigarette
between her lips!

She is herself on stage—in Seville in the 1820s, in Radford, Nottingham, in 1968.

(the physics of writing)

⌒

"Look! Look! He's bleeding!"

She looks and sees a blurring. Her head grows light. Knees turn to jellied meat and all that is solid oozes.

The air is hot. Sweat seeps out, cold and clammy, you can't contain this burning. You're all skin and no bones, stretched and pierced, your skin too thin to take a joke.

"Look! Look! He's bleeding!"

She feels a sensation of cutting. Cut adrift from her body, she's falling through space. She unravels sluggishly, in bits and pieces she spirals—a vortex of torpidity. Out in the void a vacuous magnet circles. Into its orbit she wants to be drawn. No more falling: nothing that falls in falls out of the big black hole.

"What's the matter?"

Neither in nor out, I *am* a black hole. Massive, an embryonic mass of burning embers, I contract, act on a lethal impulse to attract and be attracted all at once. I almost radiate, almost am a Catherine wheel, but on the edge of sanity energy evaporates, drains away in a flash, into thin air. Almost ignited, but on the edge of darkness, light is seized, dragged back inside, I'm a mass of matter trapping light. Shrinking, I grow heavier and heavier, a leaden mass collapsing inward. I'm stripped, gravity pulls me, layer after layer I'm pulled inward, a bride stripped bare by gravity. Imploding, a black hole spinning. I'm nothing. But a hole in space.

"What's the matter?"

No matter, no matter at all.

Neither dead nor alive, or both in halves, I am a cat—Schrödinger's cat, half dead and half alive, a mangy moggy molting at the speed of light.

It's touch-and-go, you touch it goes, I can't locate what kills—those murderous intentions, they dodge dimension; in relation to my body, they dissimulate, bear no relation, only grudges: they are moving points in a catastrophic space.

Then, though it happens imperceptibly, shadows take shape in the dark, a vague sensation of pain infiltrates the atmosphere. Slowly it finds a spot, this ghostly sense of pain, becomes attached and settles. It's somewhere, she realizes, not everywhere but *somewhere*—in my body. It has a place, this pain, it hovers almost beyond reach and then composes. I move minutely and feel resistance—the ground coheres and fears of falling, fears of flying forever, start to dissipate. I stretch my fingers and feel the ground, feel the contours of a world beyond the body.

"What's the matter?"

She holds out her hand and something is placed there. She registers its shape, feels its density, how it nestles in her palm. She holds it in one hand between her thumb and forefinger, and with the other hand runs her fingers along its length. If ink would flow from here, she thinks, the story would never end. "Give me a light," she says. She feels it in her mouth, feels the heat as a lighter's flicked and the flame transferred. She inhales, deeply, feels the air flow into her lungs, nicotine rushing through her veins. And then she breathes out, very slowly, watches the smoke whoosh from her mouth in a cloud, resolving into tendrils that twist and twirl and undulate and then abate. Peacefully. She holds the cigarette up against the sky, sees it separate from her body. She can inhale, draw smoke into her body, and she can exhale, breathe that same smoke out into the world. There's an inside and an outside, and between there is smoke and the mobility of breath.

WRITING, like smoking, delineates the body. Writing is matter, it moves, it is antimatter in motion. But what takes place between the mouth and the page? What spaces open up, what monstrous shapes emerge unbidden? Spitting, vomiting, seething, scratching, craving, stabbing in the dark—these are the tics and bodily tropes that impel a practice we might call "inscribbling." In the process of inscribbling, words are processed, bodies healed, refined. Refined, some might say, out of existence.

I often wonder why, when the body is jolted, when it resorts to jotting and doodling, why—when the world is bereft of images and aphasia threatens engulfment—why then is it an inapt and alien tongue that murmurs, random words of scientific decorum that surface from the murky depths of a dark forgotten continent. Physics tells us little of comfort about bodies—living bodies, that is, the matter we're made of. As far as we're concerned—you and I, the human population—it's the side effects of a certain scientific theory that we register. Quantum physics in the twentieth century has paved the way for the dying trade or, if you like, the futures market; theories of predictability have assured the viability of insurance companies. Even though it is impossible to predict when any particular individual will die, insurance companies, drawing on methods derived from calculating the behavior of particles, can construct reliable mortality tables. They can estimate how many people, after smoking how many cigarettes for so many years, will die when. And then according to the odds, you pay your dues. The path to superannuation is paved with good statistics. And, anyway, the bottom line for physics, what matters in the end, is not the human factor but a feline fellow traveler. You can make mincemeat of a hypothetical cat with less compunction. The reaction, though, is no less lethal if you posit a human in a sealed container with a decaying particle of radioactive matter and a vial of poison. But it is far less thinkable and the words to say it are the words of war.

As a science of the body physics is inept, but under duress these words from an alien register recur, murmuring the body in accents curiously apt. It is not in its certainty but in its failures of logic, its proliferation of paradoxes, that it fights the terrifying phantoms of aphasia. It remains to me mysterious how bodies of all sorts, of organs and of thoughts, materialize in writing. But as for the poetics of psychosis, or physics as some might call it, I think it has to do with doubt, not knowledge. Despite all calculus, it's the *not knowing* that makes writing happen. Not knowing what makes matter. What makes this, for instance, rather than that, matter (so much)?

HEALTHY

⌒

It is two o'clock in the morning, freezing cold, in Glasgow.
She is walking home alone, merry, warmed by food and wine
and good company. It is very quiet; all good citizens are in
their beds and only the *tsotsis* are abroad, roaming the Glasgow night, hiding behind lampposts, poised to leap out as she
passes. She's alert to danger, walks wide of the pavement,
making sure that in the event of an encounter, she will not be
hedged in. Turning onto a new street, she makes sure not to
hug the corner but to circle outward, making space to meet
her enemy face-to-face, clearing a path in case she needs to
make a run for it.

Tingling, skin scratched by needles of ice, she plunges her
hands into deep warm woolen pockets. In one pocket her
hand closes around a pack of cigarettes, in the other around
a lighter. Immediately she feels warmer, safer, anticipates arriving home, where the gas fire will be on and the room will
be toasty; she will undress and put on her silk pajamas, pour
a small scotch and light up a cigarette, lie back and listen to
Frank Sinatra. As she fondles the cigarette pack, a slight murmur, a rhythmical beat, intrudes on her consciousness. She
stiffens and imperceptibly quickens her pace, trying to walk
with a less heavy tread so that she can work out whether it is
simply the echo of her own footsteps or whether she is being
tracked. The sound grows louder, coming not from behind,
but toward her. Through the darkness and dull light of the
street lamp she can eventually make out a figure: a large figure, a man in a huge overcoat, approaching her on the same
side of the street. Instantly summoning all the midnight nonchalance she can, she crosses to the other side, never faltering

in her pace, and even though she is tempted to speed up—to start running even, to run and scream like a banshee through the silent streets, waking the sleeping citizens all around—she doesn't. She walks in a measured way, looking straight ahead. They approach one another, on opposite sides of the street, and she knows that this space could be traversed in an instant. Drawing closer his footsteps slow and he seems to veer ever so slightly toward her. And then he speaks. Across the Rubicon he addresses her: "'Scuse me, Hen, but you wouldn't happen to have a cigarette to spare, would you?" Without thinking she replies, a reply that is pure reflex, his question returned like a ball, kicked straight back: "Sorry, I don't smoke." As she says this her hand tightens around the cigarette pack, squishing the cigarettes, tobacco spilling into her pocket. She puts her head down slightly, fighting her way into the cold, trying not to look at him, to keep going at a steady pace. They pass.

After half a minute maybe, she becomes aware of his footsteps faltering ever so slightly, he pauses for a moment and turns, she can hear his heel swivel thirty degrees, and she feels the retort he hurtles over his shoulder, feels it fly through space and into her body. "Well, good for you, lass," he says. "You must be very healthy."

STRANGE ATTRACTORS

In the dark, about to knock gently on the windowpane, she pauses. Inside there is light, the sound of voices, conviviality. In this house she used to spend a lot of time, time spent smoking cigarettes, taking things for granted. She hasn't been here lately, too much smoke hanging in the atmosphere, in-filtrating friendship. Now, outside the window, she's wishing for things to be the way they were: she wants to trade stories, to confess and be absolved and to smoke in company. She lifts her hand to knock gently on the windowpane, anticipating all the pleasures of recovery. But at the very instant when this anticipation is most vivid—she can smell nothing but smoke, feel the cigarette between her fingers, the ecstasy of inhalation—something within her resists gratification. Violently. In self-defense she clenches, forms a fist, and strikes a blow.

Blood is dripping onto splintered glass, there are people around her, the smell of antiseptic, soothing murmurs. She is scornful of their solicitude, their complicity in her debasement. "I don't want your pity," she says, "just give me a drink." Drinks are poured and they sit around a table littered with after-dinner debris. She'd like to relinquish her bandaged hand, find somewhere to put it, but there are no spaces. In front of her an ashtray has overflowed, cigarette butts float in the oily remnants of a salad dressing.

She feels like the ghost of Elijah, a parsimonious and re-criminating presence at the dinner table. While refusing all that is offered, she covets almost everything—everything that has been consumed in her absence: strawberry ice cream, blue-veined cheese, shrimp pâté, spaghetti sauce, cigarettes.

She makes a silent vow: to sip her drink slowly, to practice self-effacement.

Around the table there is silence. "This is the end," she says. "I'm through with him." Around the table there is silence, falling like tinkling glass. They look at her, compassionately, reserving judgment, saying nothing. She perceives a pattern, sees them knitting in unison, a Fair Isle moral emerging. Cigarettes are passed around, pass her by, she demands a drink, berates them: "In my hour of need where were you? Where were you when I stood accused, without defense, where were you then, my friends? Saving up the little acts of treachery, all those little acts accumulating, adding up with interest, waiting for the big withdrawal." She looks around the table and tells them: "When I need you most, where are you?"

Someone says: "After all, when all is said and done, and when it finally comes down to it, and the cards are on the table, and the writing's on the wall, let's face it, anyone can see you have a little habit, a compulsion to repeat."

"Tell me more, tell me more," she says.

"I know what you're thinking," she says. "You think they're all the same, these men, or rather should we say these boys—pretty boys, the ones with pretensions to malice, the lethal ones, intravenous lovers, rebels dedicated to a cause, to making misery while the moon shines. For you it's everything in moderation, cut and trim the excess, shop around and put your mouth where your money is in safe deposits, package deals, tailor desire to suit the circumstances, practice Tayloristic passion if at all."

"Catastrophe recurs," someone says.

She answers: "Catastrophe is never the same twice. But how could you know, you with your compulsion for comfort, for the Swiss army drug that cuts no ice with parabolic orbits. You yearn for visual rectitude, for straight lines that intersect, Euclidean congruence a model for the interpersonal. Never in your wildest dreams could you imagine strange attraction—the elegant oscillations, febrile intricacies, iterations of difference."

As she speaks she feels the slipperiness of words, their tendency to sudden slurring; and at the same time she marvels at their magic, how they unfurl and string together, despite the slowness of her mind. She looks around the table and sees an audience enraptured, drinking in her every word; their attention intoxicates. Words, words, their autocatalytic propensity . . .

She begins to detail his difference, to count his ways, to re-count the ways in which she loves him, how he gives her something she needs . . . gave her . . . loved . . . something . . . she still needs.

In this hour of need she understands—an understanding that hits her with the apparent force of primal acumen—that suffering extenuates time and time intensifies suffering. All paradox is reduced to this: I am, therefore no exit.

One drink leads to another, and another, till discretion disperses—everything flows and you never sip from the same drink twice. Swept away, she is nevertheless aware that this fictive river of no return is taking on a life of its own, taking her on board as a character, invested with all the lushly duplicitous veracity of firsthand experience. Storytelling lights her up, instead of lighting a cigarette (in order to see in the dark and be seen), she sets fire to a field of words. She douses them, dry as tinder, in alcohol and they catch light. One at a time to begin with, just a few words on the periphery of vision, and then the flames spread, and she is illuminated, in the center of the bonfire, like Joan of Arc. And everyone around her is warmed.

Or laughing. She has a sense, even in this moment of transcendence, of something out of sync, as though she's miscalculated, got the timing wrong, overdosed publicly on that most terrible and banal of drugs—the self. The sound of canned laughter spills into the scene and the image of herself as Falconetti, beautiful and tragic, is displaced by that of a ditzy redhead—as loud as Falconetti's Joan is silent.

Lucy, in her most sublime rendition of the sudsy sitcom diva, gets a job (a rather humiliating job for an aspiring star of stage and screen) advertising cough syrup on television. She has to take a sip and extol the medicine's virtues. Well, one sip leads to another, for the cough syrup is copiously laced with alcohol, and one word leads to another, to a veritable avalanche of words, to an operatic and utterly incoherent babble.

The episode will end of course. But then there will be another episode in which Lucy is compelled by those tenacious domestic demons to act out, for a canned audience, another deliriously wordy scenario of self-immolation.

A LYCANTHROPIC AGE

(the writing cure)

∞

For hours I sit here—scribbling, chasing words, breathless.
My stomach gurgles, petulant and painful. I imagine eating
but know that if I move away from this desk, that's the very
moment when they'll all conspire: eel-like explanations ellip-
soidal, intricated metaphors crepuscular, and death-defying
flights of crinkum-crankum logic. "Hang on, mate," you'll
say, "who the hell d'you think y'are—Harold Holt waiting for
a wave? Now listen, mate—yes, you, you're the one I'm talking to—*you* are an agent of change." Well, if we're talking of
agency—and why not, in this day and age, agency is an ontological sine qua non—just remember this: for every agent,
there's a gang, a dopple too, but two can play (at double
cross). Just never leave your desk, and if you go down to the
end of the town, never go alone and never accept jelly words
from strange smokers in ruined coats. Take your muse if you
go, but better still lie low, concupiscent and vulpine. Listen to
the lullaby lunarian and wait: and the time will come, a lycanthropic age, when you will lick your chops and find your
appetite. Transmogrified. Not now monocular. Now: de-
praved and multifarious, a miracle of modern musery.

But beware the mongrel muse. She rambles and her mutterings though sibilant may well be murderous. She writes me
off the page, I am tossed and I am lost in her tumble-dryer
arms. There's a tremble in the air and a troubled premonition, I must write and I must write for at my back I always
hear:

nic-o-tine-nic-o-tine-nic-o-tine

hauntering near.

Stop and think for a moment:

What will happen if I stop writing? Will the words all disappear forever, sucked back into some primitive vortex, where they all revert to savagery and snarl and feed on one another? Will I, deprived of what keeps me going, become catatonic? Or will I babble mad and maudlin like Ophelia: remember me, dismember me, and lick the blood from my words. Or worse still, the final act for which these others are just a rehearsal, a curtain raiser. Will I internally combust, go up in smoke?

Something curious is happening. Writing is now a guarantee of not-smoking just as smoking, once upon a time, was a guarantee of writing. Both guarantees (as forms of insurance, fetishistically contractual) are neurotic, symptomatic of obsession.

Yet to say this, write this, does nothing to alleviate the terror of not-smoking, its association with not-writing.

Writing per se? Perhaps, but then again . . . I've become attached to this particular tract. Attachment literalized, I'm in traction, my body's breath is drawn along the surface of the page, everything is surface, an absence of verso. I am written into this writing. A new addiction, compelling, all-consuming. Through a process of reversal it's become a way of avoiding smoking—but more significant than this, it's become a deviously ironic method for avoiding writing itself. That is to say: any writing other than itself.

A BOIL ABOUT TO BURST

(the talking cure)

∞

The silence stretched, minutes ticked by, half an hour passed. Lying back on the sticky leatherette couch, deeply bored, she gazed at the ceiling and imagined she was H. D., reclining on an oriental rug, watching smoke rings from Freud's cigar swirling in the air over her head. For a moment she *was* H. D., breathing in the atmosphere of that marvelous room, exchanging witty and learned insights with the man himself. O to be so lucky! For her it was just long stretches of silence, tedium, lying in an off-white room with artificial cream-colored flowers and an old man devoid of acumen and humor, totally unskilled in the art of repartee. A shrink manqué, she'd recently decided, which made of her a fool, or at the very least a faux neurotic.

Though it hadn't always been that way. In the beginning, when she'd started making these daily trips, her life had been unexpectedly charged with significance, her own existence suddenly appeared to her mysterious, even fascinating in a slightly repulsive way, like a boil about to burst. She had talked and cried endlessly, day after day she'd reenacted and scrutinized the awful abjection of her dependency. And while she was lying there each day, babbling on or sobbing or choking back emotion or letting it all hang out, the aching need had left her. It was as though in the process of remembering, of scraping away the past and gathering up all the splintered remnants of nicotine sensation, her body was miraculously cleansed of craving. For the twenty-three hours when she wasn't there, she would luxuriate in scenarios of anticipation, rehearse confessions; she'd imagine in minute detail his responses, and hone her replies, cut her rapier retorts to the measure of his desire. She'd speculate about his tastes, his reading habits, and his sexual preferences. Then, as the fantasies became alarmingly lurid, she'd be consumed by jealousy—even though "it clearly isn't *him* I want," she'd tell herself. Waiting, always waiting for and wanting the next session, time passed furiously.

Then she started to run out of things to say, her feelings seemed unaccountably less intense, or maybe more banal. Certainly less appetizing. Nevertheless she tried and prattled on about this and that: her cat and its mating habits, the mediocrity and grayness of her colleagues, Pritikin diets, the boring boys she should have married but didn't. She moaned in a halfhearted way about how she always seemed to miss the boat, how happiness—or call it satisfaction—had a desultory knack of evading her, of sailing past as she stood shivering on the pebbly shore.

After a while something impinged on her prattling, a niggling sense of something missing. It was his voice, she realized. True, he had never been a lively interlocutor, but in the past she could expect and even relish his occasional laconic interceptions. Now her revelations and ruminations meandered through space, evading all contact with the outer world, coming home untransformed, to roost. And fester. She began to grow anxious, to inject her monologues with casual questions and purposeful pauses. To no avail. Then one day as she lay there wondering what to say next, there was a rippling in the air, as though a cat were purring next door or a water pipe were spluttering somewhere down the corridor. She held herself very still and listened intently. Could it be her imagination? Surely it could not be, it could not be what she thought it was. The more she listened to the sound, the more it sounded horribly familiar. Unmistakably someone in the room was snoring.

Flushed with embarrassment, she contemplated sliding

squeakily off the dove-gray leatherette couch and sneaking across the mushroom pink semiwool carpet and out the door. Never to return to that off-white room filled with the sounds of silence and snoring. But then something twitched in her stomach, something like a tweak of hunger or even an intimation of craving. As it grew and rose up in her being, she realized that this sensation was a simple one: it was unadulterated anger. She sat up and did the unthinkable—she turned and looked her shrink in the face. It was an old and crumpled face, but even in snatched and ignominious repose, it had an air of authoritarian aloofness.

"Excuse me," she said, "but I was talking."

"Goodness me," he said, "I must have dozed off."

Tears started streaming down her face, furious tears, the tears of a woman scorned. "How could you! How could you do this to me—you pretend to be interested and all the while you aren't even listening. Well, that I could forgive actually—we all have other things on our mind now and then—but to fall asleep, to snore while I'm talking to you! Not to mention paying you! Am I really that boring?"

"Well, since you ask, frankly my dear, yes," he said.

Silence for a long time. She was stunned by his familiar form of address, his use of the affectionate epithet: *my dear* reverberated in the air, circling between them just like the smoke rings eddying between Freud and H. D.

"Have you always felt this way?" she asked eventually. "Have you always found me boring?"

"Not at all. There was a time when you told a cracking good story, kept me on my toes. But you seem to have lost the knack; the heart's gone out of you. Perhaps you don't care anymore to keep my interest."

She was aghast. "I'm here to entertain you? I'm paying you for the privilege?"

"In a manner of speaking, yes. If you want returns. Incidentally, I wonder why you used that phrase: 'me boring'?"

"Me Boring, You Tarzan."

"Touché. Lie down, Jane," he said, almost cracking a smile, "and tell me a story."

For a while things had picked up—she'd lifted her game and, spurred on by acrimony, had exercised some ingenuity. Her stories became more and more risqué, and although he showed no visible appreciation, she took his staying awake as a positive sign. He wants to be interested, she told herself. He's interested, he says, but in what I wonder is he interested? Is it the tales I tell that lure him, or could it be—more fundamentally—me? Or is it the same old story: it's just my mind he wants, he doesn't crave my body?

This thought induced a new stage in the proceedings—a dull and chronic despondency on her part, matched by an apparent empathy on his. There was no more snoring, but also no sense of need, no trading of insults nor clandestine and deliciously heretical flirtation. She said less and less, and he responded in kind. You could almost say (as you'd say of couples still together though long long past it) they shared a comfortable silence. Except that she was deeply bored. Lying there, imagining H. D. and the smoke rings, once again wanting more than anything to smoke herself, she thinks: the grass is greener, the shrinks are younger and more enticing over there. Time to switch horses, time to give this old man the push.

Just at that point, suddenly and uncharacteristically, out of the blue, he told her something about himself.

"I've been married twice, you know."

The first time, he told her, was for about ten years. Many of those were good years, but then his wife began drinking, quickly turned into an alcoholic, and refused advice or treatment. She would become very violent in her drinking bouts, and he would often lie in his bed at night, rigid with terror. Then later he married again, and for the first three years or so he was blissfully happy. But then this second wife became severely depressed and refused not only therapy but also antidepressant drugs.

She is struck by two things in this saga of marital misfortune. First, both the wives suffer from what he describes as organic disorders, and, second, he has nothing to do with their illnesses. This immediately affirms her resolve to dump him. Though of course she says nothing, just lies back and looks at the ceiling.

There is a long silence and then he says, "Actually, I rather fumbled my marriages."

Unaccountably she is touched. It is the word *fumbled* that does it, that insinuates a hairline crack in the certainty of her decision to leave. She thinks: Oh well, I'll stay a little longer.

A week after this he dropped dead. She arrived one morning to find a notice on the door saying ALL APPOINTMENTS CANCELED TODAY. And forever more, as she soon discovered. Devastated, she turned around and went home, and on the way she bought a pack of cigarettes, and began again.

VOICING

There's a genre of which I partake—the writing-through-addiction genre. Writing as enabled by addiction; and its obverse: writing through it as in a thriller, driving through a roadblock, coming out the other side. This genre is destined to be diaristic, tediously personal, acutely experiential. This is the voice that voices vice. A voice that resonates the sensory, years of roll-your-own and scotch, throaty, self-indulgent, writing the blues. A conventional voice. Roll your own: you've made your bed, now lie on it. But I don't want to sleep alone. And so I must write for someone else. I write to elicit recognition, for the pleasure of sharing the illicit. Though you're all alone when you go through it (it's not called withdrawal for nothing), paradoxically it's an unutterably common, profoundly cultural experience. Unvoiced, though. Somatized as eccentricity. Those repressed gestures of the voice emerge as temperamental snarls, idiosyncratic whines, and murderously solipsistic mutterings. To engender a voice— gravelly, generically traced by its own dissolution: this is to not-give-up.

MOUTHING

She was three years old and watched fixated, for hours, as blood poured out of her father's mouth.

She knew that once they reached home the bleeding would stop, but even though they drove fast—away from town, toward the farm—nothing changed, the dusty brown landscape never varied and the dirt road stretched endlessly into the distance. She sat in the front (a rare privilege) next to her mother, who was driving. By peering around the seat, she could see her father lying in the back of the car, holding a handkerchief up to his mouth. She imagined the old farmhouse—immense, implacable, and comforting with its graying thatched roof and whitewashed walls; but even as she conjured it into existence, she could see it shrinking, contracting to nothing. This is how she came to understand the phrase "to bleed to death." He held a handkerchief up to his mouth and as it grew red and sodden he grunted like a hostage, bound and gagged. "Don't try to talk," her mother said as she groped in her handbag (all the while driving, her eyes on the road ahead) for another hankie, small and flimsy, embroidered white on white.

When her father had told her, early that morning, that they were going to town to visit the dentist, who was going to pull all his teeth out, she was deeply envious, imagining all the money he would get from the tooth fairy. Now in the car so far from home she feels remorse, as though her envy has animated these butchering demons of retribution.

SHE WANTS TO put something in her mouth, too.

HE USED TO say to my mother when she raged, "Belt up, Misery Guts!" Or to us kids when we screamed and yelled: "Put a sock in it!"

"I gave them gold coins, and they ate the coins and made themselves ill," Columbus said.

COLUMBUS NARRATES in his diary the following incident: when he first encountered the natives (on coming ashore, having discovered a new land that would come to be known as America), he wished to demonstrate his goodwill and so offered them evidence of his pacific intentions, in the form of a gift. But they did not understand the principles of exchange. He says something like "for when I showed them swords they did grasp them by their blades and so did cut themselves." The person from whom I heard this story interpreted Columbus's actions not so much as military or political, but as a series of *speech* acts. He saw this narration as a proclamation, and stressed the way that Christopher Columbus is constantly declaring, witnessing, recording. Perhaps this is so, but on hearing this story I was immediately struck by something else, some other reverberation. I was struck by the act of disavowal.

You put a cigarette in your mouth to stop the bleeding, as a stopgap measure, to plug the hole and stop the blood from pouring out.

Even though you know his teeth have been drawn, his flashing smile is false, you are still afraid. Perhaps you are afraid precisely—or imprecisely—*because* you know this. And so you turn your fear to pleasure and light up another cigarette. And write a story.

⌒

A young child—perhaps three or four years old—sucks on his mother's breast. He removes his mouth from her nipple and turns to face us, lips still parted. Almost immediately he lifts a cigarette to his mouth, sucks, and then blows the smoke indifferently into the camera. Then he smiles.

This scene (from the film *Mother Dao, the Turtlelike*) invariably provokes a shocked reaction. Everyone remembers it, can describe it in detail, in tones of fascinated horror. Is it horror, I wonder, at the infant smoking, or the mixing of substances—of mother's milk with poison? Or is it revulsion at something perceived as not quite human? The open mouth: insatiable greed, untempered orality.

Whence the narrow constipation of a strictly human attitude, the magisterial look of the face with a **closed mouth,** as beautiful as a safe. — GEORGES BATAILLES, "MOUTH"

The postcoital smoke, the after-eating drag, the aprés ocean inhalation—I always used to think of these as a kind of capping off or maybe even a winding out, of ecstasy, a way of making the pleasure last. But maybe they're the obverse, more like a defense against excess. When the meal becomes truly luscious, when there's a richness that oozes through the boundary between courses, that's when I start craving a cigarette. For a spurt of fresh lime juice over congealing oil. Lighting up a cigarette is akin to lighting the candles of appeasement, like you have to counteract indulgence by enacting atonement, through a ritual of purification. It's as though when you exhale smoke you expel all the food that's taken in. Some people leave the table, stick a couple of fingers down their throats and throw up, then come back and have a second helping of chocolate cake. Other people light up between courses and spill the ash over the remnants of feasting, stub their cigarettes out in a saucer smeared already by chocolate icing.

What goes in must come out. Smoking and eating are thus 135 connected in a certain bodily economy regulated through orality. Storytelling too: listening, we submit to a state of relaxation, the story is absorbed into our own experience, woven into the fabric of personal memory, and it is this process of assimilation that enables the story to be repeated.

> Men and women and children would gather about me when I smoked. The leader of these uninvited guests came close enough to inhale the smoke as it was ejected. For a few moments he retained it, then blew it into the mouth of a companion, the process being continued until each had received a puff, or the smoke was exhausted. — A EUROPEAN TRAVELER IN AFRICA, CA. 1890

Or raw experience is absorbed, assimilated, and somehow processed to emerge transformed, as a story, there to circulate in the social. Though in the circulation the story may be blown hither and thither, and when you begin with that oft-repeated phrase "once upon a time" in fact you can never be certain where subsequent repetitions will take your telling. Other people may eat your gift, your words, and regurgitate, render unrecognizable, your meanings.

So, yes, what goes in must come out, but between the going in and coming out, things happen. Magical processes, processes of conversion. The process of conversion, however, is more often than not tricky rather than straightforward. Substances seldom convert into other substances in a direct way, just as desires, though they may mutate, seldom substitute neatly one for another. Today, in what we call our culture, eating is seen primarily as a matter of consumption, of self-replacement, of nourishment. And smoking is seen almost as the obverse—as self-destruction, an instance of excessive consumption. But there are other cultures, such as the Melanesian, where eating is not a simple matter of self-replacement, nor primarily a process of consumption. Since knowledge is located in the stomach, eating constitutes a kind of production, what might be thought of as "consumptive production"—what is being produced in the exchange and consumption of foods is knowledge, and knowledge is only "known" through being consumed.

> *"I gave them gold coins, and they ate the coins and made themselves ill," Columbus said.*

Absorbing and testing a foreign currency, it seems the Native Americans found it wanting, and so they regurgitated that alien culture. In Tsitsi Dangarembga's *Nervous Conditions*, Nyasha, the Shona girl who has been "whited"—so thoroughly educated in a European system that she has lost her own Shona language and traditions—tears her history book to shreds with her teeth. She is at once eating or consuming this knowledge and spitting it out.

Sucking on a cigarette is akin to sucking at the mother's breast. But in the juxtaposition of these activities, there might also be a confusion, an incongruity between what goes in and what comes out. Freud shows how the antagonism of projection and introjection is expressed in the oldest of languages, in the oral-instinctual impulses. The judgment is: "I should like to eat this" or "I should like to spit it out." When there is a confusion between what to take in and what to keep out, between pleasure and unpleasure, then there is an introjection of unpleasurable objects. This kind of introjection characterizes conditions like melancholia or depression—which are linked to oral incorporation, even though it is not necessarily food or even objects per se that are taken in (despite a desire to spit things out). Words can function as a kind of melancholic food: in a perversion of storytelling unpleasant sentiments and recalcitrant nasty words, instead of being uttered, are incorporated into the body, where they brood and feed on one another. So it is with Nyasha, who suffers from a performative "illness" that we call bulimia. Eating disorders are often conceived of as self-destructive, as a refusal of nourishment and self-replacement. But there's another way of looking at them: as an active and social refusal, an inability to stomach aspects of an alien culture (that is sometimes, also, one's own culture), a struggle for the expulsion of a foreign body that has taken possession of one's own being. A kind of cultural melancholia, and as such a form of "consumptive production"—a recognition and monitoring of relationships.

The process of conversion—between what goes in and what comes out, between food and vomit, smoke and smoke, and also between the self and the social—is more often than not a tricky one. Without the gifts of a *n'anga* or a *freud* it's easy to be deceived; take the case of the withered lettuce leaf. Violette Leduc's autobiographical novel *La Bâtarde* opens with a theatrical flourish, a supposedly self-effacing declaration of masochistic melancholia:

> My case is not unique: I am afraid of dying and distressed at being in this world. I haven't worked, I haven't studied. I have wept, I have cried out in protest. These tears and cries have taken up a great deal of my time. I am tortured by all that time lost whenever I think about it. I cannot think about things for long, but I can find pleasure in a withered lettuce leaf offering nothing but regrets to chew

over. There is no sustenance in the past. I shall depart as I
arrived. Intact, loaded down with the defects that have tor-
mented me. I wish I had been born a statue.

Her testimonial is a confession of melancholia and also evidence that this melancholia requires feeding. But rather than
taking in food she absorbs regrets; hunger is transformed into
depression or abject self-loathing and projected onto a potential item of food—a withered lettuce leaf. Compare this
opening with that of another famous autobiographical address:

> I have resolved on an enterprise which has no precedent,
> and which, once complete, will have no imitator. My pur-
> pose is to display to my kind a portrait in every way true to
> nature, and the man I shall portray will be myself.
>
> —ROUSSEAU, *The Confessions*

Now, for all the solipsistic tone of both these texts, the
very utterance (of the "self") constitutes a conversion; offered
as an opening gambit, a personalized confession materializes
as a story, or a rhetorical gift. In Rousseau, nature materializes
as a man, and he offers this man—himself, no less—as a gift
to the reader. In Leduc hunger materializes as a withered lettuce leaf and is offered as a gift to the reader. In both cases the
words and sentiments are let loose as a kind of recognition
and monitoring of relationships; above all else they confess to
an impulse to confession, and in doing so they implicate the
reader as accomplice in a routinized ritual of fictionality. I'm
taken in by both these texts, I take in the words and chew
them over. But there is a difference. With Leduc I find myself
inhaling the words, savoring their flavor as one savors smoke,
before blowing it out. The Rousseau makes me choke, come
close to throwing up. In Rousseau I recognize "the narrow
constipation of a strictly human attitude." In Leduc, despite
the anorexic pose, I recognize an openmouthed insatiable

greed. I find her words delicious, I want to eat that withered lettuce leaf, I take delight in the histrionic dramatization of what we may think of as a certain gendering of the gift in our so-called civilized community.

Oh, the hyperbolic bathos of that lettuce leaf! Peculiarly, it generates an appetite (for more).

L I O N S   D O N ' T   S M O K E

Somewhere out there, concealed in the long tawny grass, a lion lurks. In a moment he will pounce, with exhilarating speed the camera will spring into action, and the hunt will be captured. Through camera movement, through a series of re-framings, crucially timed cuts, the speeding up and slowing down of motion, the spectacle will unfold. We are in the realm of *Simba: The King of the Beasts*, a 1928 film shot in East Africa by the filmmakers Martin and Asa Johnson. I am en-raptured by these images of wildlife, this conjuring of an African landscape with its low and constant horizon, with the evocation of stillness and motion. The beauty of these 35 mm images amazes me, as does the enormity of the exercise—lug-ging that huge battalion of gigantic cameras across the sea and into the African bush.

As the lights come up, people start talking and moving, but I sit still for a moment, eyes closed, trying to keep the im-ages alive in the dark. After several days of watching early ac-tuality films from various colonial contexts, these images are arresting, startlingly different. I am captivated by the elegant giraffes moving in infinitesimally slow-motion across the sky-line, by the zebra splashing the landscape with brash Mary Quant designs, by the warthogs that run dementedly, their tails straight up in the air. I love to watch them all, but most of all I love Simba the lion. I adore Simba for these reasons:

he doesn't make shoes
he doesn't play the mandolin
he doesn't do ethnic dances
he doesn't get married in national costume

he doesn't cultivate tea or coffee
he doesn't smoke

What does he do? What does he do that is positive, not weighed in simply negative terms? Well, he moves divinely and elicits from the camera a mirroring and magical motion, and he seems simply to be himself—independent of my gaze—to be simply Simba the lion. The pleasure of watching these animals relieves me of a certain self-consciousness, relieves me slightly of the burden entailed by my position as a postcolonial viewer, indeed as a white colonial film critic. Although it might well be that I am merely mimicking an injunction delivered to the Johnsons: "The public is tired of savages. Get some animal pictures." This was a telegram sent by Robertson-Cole, who were marketing their films, to which the Johnsons responded by going off to Africa, and the public was reanimated, attentive again, enraptured.

Of course the sense of relief, of escape from a compromised and discomforting viewing position, is both fleeting and illusory. Even in *Simba* there is an insistent alignment of natives and animals, and of guns and cameras (though not as insistently and tyrannically staged as in *A Marriage amongst the Red Skins*, where an intertitle tells us: "In single file like geese the Tepee tribe enter the reservation"). There is a tension between actuality and fiction, traced in the way that the drama of the lion hunt is staged and unfolds (in the denouement Simba is killed by the white woman with a gun rather than by the African men with their native spears).

It is, however, true to say that Simba is not scrutinized in precisely the same way as the "savage" is; that is to say, Simba does not bear the burden of the gaze in quite the same way, and neither does he look back. It is by now something of a truism to say that in these films the colonial gaze objectifies the other, is totalitarian in its objectification, rendering the other powerless—for to be under the scrutiny of the camera is much like being in the line of fire, at the mercy of the gun.

This is not untrue, but it sometimes simplifies and miscon-
strues, I suspect, the range of transactions involved not only
in the act of reading images, but in the very process of filming. One critical response to what has become a repetitive orthodoxy is to shift attention to the agency of the filmed, and
rather than looking for endless examples of subjugation and
objectification, to try to be more alert to signs of resistance, to
the way in which the savage looks back, often in disconcerting
ways. Two instances from the program of films in which
Simba is screened spring to mind. First, in *Mother Dao, the
Turtlelike* (a compilation of early actuality footage from the
former Dutch East Indies) a young child, perhaps three or
four years old but still suckling on his mother's breast, removes his mouth, turns to face us, lips still parted, and almost
immediately lifts a cigarette, sucks, and then blows the smoke
indifferently into the camera. Second, in *Among the Cannibal
Isles of the South Pacific* (1917), a group of black men float past
on a canoe, they are heavily armed and they stare at the camera, a look hard to decipher—could it be indifference, contempt? They are heavily armed with rifles and belts of ammunition, and the subtitle asks: "Which unscrupulous traders
could have armed these bloodthirsty tribes . . . ?" Though
earlier in the film we have been told that the filmmakers
themselves "equipped our men with repeating rifles by way of
precaution."

In both these scenes, there is a look *at* the camera that
seems on the face of it to unsettle the normal relations of
viewing. But also in both scenes there is almost a staging of
the look, and this staging involves a certain scenic theatricalization and deployment of props: cigarettes and guns. The
scene from *Mother Dao* is shocking and usually elicits a reaction of fascinated horror; it is frequently discussed in terms of
untempered orality, of the mixing of substances—of mother's
milk with poison. But actually there is a quite different way to
apprehend the dynamics of this image, and that is to see the
cigarette (and by extension, the guns and the ammunition) as

a plant. Or at least as an index of relationality. They may be a plant in the sense of an object inserted, designed to elicit a reaction—planted, that is, by the filmmakers to elicit a performance; or they may constitute a plant in the sense of a bribe or even payment—in order to secure cooperation for filming.

All filmic processes involve transactions: a variety of relations need to be established before filming commences, and sometimes filmmaking halts when cooperation ceases or coercion fails. We can read these films as tracing symptomatically (and sometimes quite overtly) a network of sometimes shifting transactional relations.

Among the Cannibal Isles clearly and somewhat naively gives away its own game. The filmmakers make drama out of the fact that some irresponsible people have armed the savages, but they also reveal that they have given guns to chosen natives whom they wish to use as allies, entrées into the jungle, informants. They differentiate their own practice of gift giving from that of the unscrupulous traders, but actually all we can tell here is that there is a system of trading. Tobacco, guns, and cloth—as objects of exchange—all occur in *Among the Cannibal Isles*. Why should we assume that the filmmaking process lies outside this economy, particularly when these early actuality filmmakers were preceded by generations of explorers, traders, and missionaries, all of whom were, above all else, traders. The natives seldom sat back and let the foreign devils help themselves to whatever they wanted—there was always a price to pay, an agreement to be figured out, an arrangement to be made. This trading relation that preexists the films then, that circulates in the social, might also be registered through and in the films themselves. The look at the camera, the blowing of smoke into the audience, may then function to say something like this: "OK, I've been paid to do this, and so I am doing it, but not for fun, not for your unmitigated pleasure." So they are right, those who detect a resistance, but it is at least possible that this resistance is traced by a complex circuitry, by a system of objects that circulate between people, between both sides of the camera, and between films.

Tobacco and guns may not then be the most privileged objects of exchange. But then again, they might. And perhaps, after all, Simba does smoke.

POISON

∞

NO SMOKING INDOORS PLEASE

First there are directions for getting to the beach shack, directions that guide you lucidly out of metropolitan Sydney, through green rolling pastures and *melaleuca* forests, to a wild and windswept promontory. There, perched in magnificently photogenic isolation, on the edge of a cliff, is the shack. It is a cunningly insulated, thickly carpeted house, well stocked with Le Creuset pots and pans, an espresso maker and a coffee plunger, a vacu-seal pump for wine bottles, a food processor, two carving knives, no ashtrays. The directions proceed: how to operate the various white goods in the house, how and where to dispose of rubbish, what to do if the red light gleams on the vacuum cleaner, how to deal with snakes. And then it says, as though in afterthought: NO SMOKING INDOORS PLEASE. It is the "please" that she finds most irksome—posing as an intimation of courtesy, it actually gives the lie to the afterthought, indicates that this is a request that has been brooded over, nurtured through a long malevolent winter, burnished into being during a deep-sustaining depression, delivered with self-effacing malevolence. "Hey, You!" it says. "Don't Do It!" It is a royal prohibition.

She is with five other people, all of whom read the polite request, nod in unison, and chant, "Of course." They do not smoke. They have all brought a lot of books and a lot of bottles of wine. She has brought a suitcase full of cigarettes. They all start reading in bed early in the morning, snuggling up to one another, and only open the wine after the sun has set and the pasta sauce is bubbling on the hob. She rises late each day and sits on the deck upstairs with her prebreakfast pot of coffee and opens a new pack of cigarettes. She lights up, inhales, exhales. Smoke whooshes and sails in rings over the ocean, lassoing the white horses that toss their manes and somersault and tear out of the water into the sky. At night after the others have vacu-sealed the wine bottle, washed the dishes, and retired, she takes the bottle onto the deck, pops open the vacu-seal, lines up her last cigarettes for the day, and by the light of the silvery moon applies her velvety shimmering lipstick. She sips and smokes slowly, the sound of the surf and the wind through the eucalypts wraps around her like a goose-down quilt. Ideas and images percolate.

There are no ashtrays in the house.

On the first day she searches for a substitute and eventually finds an empty jar, scrubbed scrupulously clean, though the label has been preserved—a simple label, in black and white, no illustrations. It reads:

pastabilities
shiitake mushrooms, sun-dried tomatoes,
cream and white wine sauce

At the end of the holiday, her pastabilities jar is filled with ash and crumpled cigarette butts and lipstick traces—bright purply red splashes.

She says she will make the last supper, and so on the final day of the holiday, she travels far afield to gather her thoughts and her ingredients. She returns with a tin of tomatoes and some dilapidated button mushrooms and a carton of thickened cream, preservatives added. She whips all this up in the food processor with the contents of the pastabilities jar and sautés the purée lightly in olive oil and mushrooms and white wine. Finally she tosses the pasta in this sauce, sprinkles the platter with parsley and Reggiano parmesan, and serves it up.

FOG DRINKING

It's Saturday afternoon in Makokoba Township in Bulawayo. Everyone is out on the streets, meandering and exchanging greetings, or sitting and chatting, or kicking balls around, or buying or selling. Nothing exactly seems to be happening and yet there is movement in the air, an atmosphere of charged indolence, dramas brewing. Men and women sit on the pavement selling all sorts of things—bright red chilies, greens of various kinds, tomatoes, sweets, ballpoint pens, cellophane plastic packets of flaky tobacco, large cones of dingy brown tobacco leaf trussed up in red wool, *amacimbi* (dried caterpillar), spices, nuts, beer. Every so often I hear the word *ikhiwa*—"white woman." "There's that white woman again," they say. I'm with my friend Sibahle, and everyone in the township knows her. Right now, as we amble through the small streets, she looks like anyone else, like any young woman out on the town on Saturday afternoon, but the truth is this: at night, on the stage, she's a star. She belongs to a wildly popular theater group, and she can sing and dance and cut through space like a dervish. But this is not the only reason that she's treated with deference—like everyone else in her group she's an ace kung fu practitioner.

We pass some young kids selling single custom-made cigarettes. I think of Sibahle's brother, who is a great comic and stage fighter, a kind of small and skinny African Jackie Chan. He, too, became an actor and this is how it happened: at fourteen he was a street vendor, just like these kids, barely eking out an existence buying and selling cigarettes. At the end of every day as he prepared to go home with his meager takings, packing up everything he hadn't sold, he'd get beaten up. And every night, after he'd been beaten up, he'd stop at the community hall on his way home and look through the window. Saturday night was the big night at the hall—when people would gather here to watch kung fu movies; but every other night of the week the hall would be occupied by the township karate class. One day it dawned on him that this might be a way to hold his own. So he joined the classes, figuring that he'd learn to fight. "Well, did it work?" I ask. "I guess it did 'cause you sure can fight." "No," he said, "I learned to act; what I learned in karate was how to talk my way out of a fight." I'm glad he watched kung fu and that the Makokoba class turned to acting, for one of the great pleasures of life in Bulawayo is to see him on the stage playing a *tsotsi* (gangster), to witness his brand of balletic burlesque, his split-second slapstick.

We stop and talk with a very old man, perched on an upturned wooden fruit crate, next to a small cottage tobacco industry. He wears tiny wire-rimmed spectacles held together by bits of string, has no front teeth left, and is smoking cigarette after cigarette rolled in newspaper and made from the tobacco that is being sold in packets and cones. He's been smoking this tobacco for a very long time. "It's strong stuff," he says, "very bad for you, but me, it keeps me alive. Sometimes though," he says, "if you smoke too much, it makes you drunk and a bit mad."

He uses the Ndebele word for *drunk* or *inebriated*, and we laugh. But this concept of drinking smoke is not uncommon. In Europe, for a long time there was simply no name for what you did with tobacco. Only in the course of the seventeenth century did "smoking" become a commonly used term. Up to that time it was compared with drinking—one spoke of "drinking smoke" and "drinking tobacco." Schivelbusch tells us that in 1627 the Palatinate's ambassador to the Netherlands reported on a new astonishing fashion there, that "might be called a fog-drinking bout. . . . Dissolute persons have taken to imbibing and noisily drinking into their bodies the smoke of a plant they call nicotiana or tobacco, with incredible avidity and inextinguishable zeal."

I can believe that this tobacco makes you drunk and, indeed, that it is slightly poisonous. It has traveled a long and circuitous route, accumulating dust and mold and a history of theft and exploitation before it reaches his lips and enters his body, there to be absorbed, there to disappear from the world. Only to reemerge in smoke and in the stories he tells. From the Tobacco Sales Rooms in Harare to the street markets of Makokoba Township in Bulawayo, stories unfurl.

The Tobacco Sales Rooms in Harare, the biggest in the world, are tumultuous, filled with movement and noise—there is continuous traffic as small motorized wagons whiz around, shipping tobacco bales in and out (ensuring that there are no gaps, no holes in space, that the floor is continuously covered from end to end by row upon row of bales); workers sweep, gathering the flakes, the dregs, the odd leaf that falls to the ground. People—prospective buyers, sellers checking out the competition—walk up and down the aisles, fingering and smelling the sample leaves that lie on top of each consignment; tourists wander around openmouthed, entranced by the secret and arcane rites performed by shamans in safari suits, auctioneers who move along the rows trailing an entourage of intent followers, comprised of the starter and two teams— buyers and sellers. The buying and selling happens in a flash: a raised eyebrow, a scratched ear, a twitching nostril—all in response to an incomprehensible though curiously hypnotic babble. The auctioneers, to save their voices, "sing" the bids; they are the center of commerce, high priests of the marketplace, sirens whose singing bewitches, attracts a trail of followers. It is a magic palace of modernity, a virtual market where—despite the fact that there is apparently no physical exchange of goods or money—commercial transactions are effected at the speed of light. It is a hazy palace shrouded in mystery and tobacco dust. As you approach the Sales Rooms, as you look from the foyer through the glass walls, you look through a haze and sense the excitement, the incipient chaos; and as you enter the space you can smell the mystery—but also feel it, heavy in the air, on your eyes, in your lungs. After a while, breathing in this atmosphere, you feel a little drunk.

A sense of chaos prevails, but in fact everything is streamlined, organized with maximum efficiency and the utmost economy. There is no wastage. Every six seconds a bale is sold, every minute up to a ton of leaf, every hour eight hundred bales.

Or no ostensible wastage.

This sense of entering a magical space is induced in part by the haze of the tobacco dust, but also by childhood memories. Thirty years collapses into nothing as I feel again the sense of excitement and anticipation, willingly lured into the siren's den. Though there are some differences. For one thing I have no personal stake now. Even then, of course, it wasn't a strictly personal stake, but holding tight to my parents, scared of getting lost in the maelstrom, I would feel the nervousness travel through their fingers as the entourage approached our bales. Time would stop for a moment, even though the singsong chanting carried on, a continuous musical babble propelled by its own cadences, oblivious to personal fortunes. Time would stop, the grip on my hand would tighten, and I would want to cry out with the pain but instead would bite my tongue—because at that moment it felt as though I were the adult and my mother was holding on to me for dear life. And so in a sense it was a matter of life or death, or to put it less dramatically, a matter of survival. And then the moment would pass, her grip would loosen, and either a charge of adrenaline would pass through our linked hands or a terrible heaviness would be transmitted. Either the horizon would open up: it would be possible to go home and write out checks, pay outstanding bills, pay the workers, give everyone a bonus—and have a celebratory breakfast, there in the canteen at the Auction Rooms, a huge meal of bacon and eggs, veined with gold, smelling of tobacco. Or the horizon would close down: the prospects would be bleak; as you cast your eyes down and scuffed through the detritus, "no future" would be written there in the tobacco dust.

And there are other differences: now it is all computerized. The electronic bulletin board flashes scarlet statistics and optimistic messages about the day's commerce and the nation's most lucrative industry (every day 20,880 kilograms are sold; from every kilogram a thousand cigarettes are made; the 1995 crop was 170 million kilograms; the expected 1996 yield was 200 million kilograms, earning about $7 billion). And another difference is that there are a lot more blacks on the floor—as auctioneers, sales reps, buyers. There are some growers too, though still the majority of growers are white. As in the old days, the men who sweep the floors and transport the bales are almost all black.

Today, as in the past, there is a peculiar tension in the air, a sense of being strung out between optimism and fatalistic dread. Here, cocooned in the hazy glasshouse of the Sales Rooms, you feel on a high, like you've reached El Dorado, like you're at the center of a booming economy; but as your eyes start stinging and everyone starts coughing, you also feel as though you're in the smoking room at the airport in Singapore—the glass room where you can go to smoke, where everyone looks in on you, trying to discern through the fog of smoke the lineaments of a dying species. Last chance for a slow dance with extinction. All this optimism is traced by another scenario enacted outside the sales yards—a drama of breakaway groups, attempts to indigenize the industry, to break the multinational and overwhelmingly white monopoly. Since early on tobacco has been the biggest revenue earner for the country, providing a continuity from Rhodesia to Zimbabwe—an identification of the country as "Tobaccoland." As a correspondent in *Africa Calls* in 1962 put it:

Australian wool, Brazilian coffee, Cuban sugar, Danish bacon, Egyptian cotton, French brandy . . . and so on through the alphabet to Rhodesian tobacco.

If any country merits identification with its principal agricultural product, Rhodesia certainly deserves to be known as "Tobaccoland."

The *African World*, as early as 1913—declaring that Rhodesia, with the cheapest land in the world and a plentiful supply of cheap labor, was perfectly suited to tobacco cultivation—concluded: "Finally, as there is no likelihood of the tobacco habit, which, in Byron's breezy words, 'from East to West cheers the tar's labour and the Turkman's rest,' becoming less prevalent in the future, there need never be any anxiety on the score of the market."

But of course Byron's breezy words, it now turns out, were truly written on the wind, and the marketplace for tobacco growers is certainly fraught with immense anxiety as the tobacco habit becomes less and less common. But for the moment bravado reigns, and all those dependent on the industry put on a brave face and continue as though little has changed. And for many it's true that little *has* changed, either in terms of smoking habits or their place within the tobacco economy, within the circuits of distribution and exchange.

I talk to the men who sweep the floor and ask them where the leftover bits and pieces go. "Are they thrown out?" I ask. No, it seems that they are collected—nothing is wasted, all the bits and pieces are sent to the graders and returned to the floors for sale. Grading is an endless and obsessive process, recurring at various points in the cycle of production. First, the leaf is graded on the farm. After it has been cured, the leaves are placed in large piles on trestle tables in the grading sheds. Every leaf has to be graded, sorted by hand according to type, size, color, and quality. The leaves are then tied in hands, with butts about one inch in diameter, the only wrapping material permissible being a tobacco leaf of identical grade. The inferior tobacco, the bits and pieces, are packed loosely into bales. Then there is further grading on the floors of the Sale Rooms, preparatory to the point of sale. "And where does the sold tobacco go?" I ask someone else. To the cigarette manufacturers, I'm told, and to the exporters. All through the industrial sites in this part of town, there are factories and warehouses dealing, one way or another, in tobacco. The debris, then, is taken from the main Sales Room, sorted and graded again, and then returned to be sold. At a certain point, after much retrieval, reintegration, resorting, grading, and selling, everyone gives up on the fallout, the unacceptable and damaged leaves, the bits of flaky splinters, the ragged mishmash. This final detritus is treated as garbage, swept away, consigned to the trash heap.

For those who wait patiently in the wings, the trash heap transmogrifies, turns to treasure. Workers in these factories, when the day is over, gather up the discarded and rejected leftovers, scoop the dregs out of the garbage bins, and stuff them into plastic rubbish bags. They sell these bags to a lower echelon of intermediaries, self-employed men who, locating themselves outside the official tobacco industry, nevertheless mirror the larger processes of accumulation and profit. They step into the breach at this point, employ their family members and others to sort again, and bag and tie and sell. Some of them transport these bags back to Bulawayo, to the streets of Makokoba. Here, in front yards and along the street on the main Luveve Road, women, and occasionally men, sit sorting again, grading the tobacco into two sorts. They sit on the ground, spreading the leaves into a fan shape and then twisting them into a cob. They stuff bits and pieces into the center, deftly twirl red wool around the cone from top to bottom, and tie. They do this in a leisurely fashion, chatting, tending to children, keeping an eye on the tin jam jar, which, set on bricks, sits at the center of each small tobacco group. In the tin, paper is burned—old newspaper, discarded wrapping paper, litter. It's relaxing work—"social work," someone tells me. The piles of leaves emptied out of the garbage bags are moistened to make them less brittle, to make the fanning and tying easier. But this means that the cobs are beginning to turn moldy, and there is a curious mixture of smells, a mingling of different tobacco odors: a musty moldy smell of slightly rotting leaves, and the dusty smell of the flaky bits that fall to the ground, get swept up with the dust, and packaged in six-inch-square plastic packets. Once the bags are filled to bulging, someone has the job of pinching the open ends together and holding the packet for a moment up against the hot tins, thus sealing it. These packets are sold for a dollar (about ten American cents) and would stretch to hundreds of cigarettes, I imagine. The cobs sell for three dollars. The vendors (who most commonly manufacture and sell in the same spot) are situated either on or close to the main Luveve Road, the road out of Bulawayo, where the bus terminal for the rural areas is located. So people stock up, buying just enough to last themselves, a spot of luxury from the city, or they will take the cones and packets back to the rural areas and sell them there for a small profit.

I am thinking about how poisonous this tobacco must be. The hunched-over old man in wire-rimmed glasses, his eyes gleaming like a chameleon's, says, "It's strong stuff, very bad for you. But I started smoking it when I was very young and now I'm very old. And I'm still alive." He looks me up and down, looks straight into my murky heart and blackened lungs: "How old are you? And how long do you think you'll live?"

KETTLE LOGIC

(the art of separation)

On the wooden chopping board there's green coriander and hot red peppers and garlic. In an offhand sort of way, distractedly, while telling me a story, you chop. I'm fascinated by the story and fixated by the chopping. So for a moment I pause at the sink; everything is suspended except a relentless gush of water flowing over a bundle of baby octopus that lie in my hands, pink and gray and tentacled. The story goes like this: you had lent him a kettle. Though he said how could you lend it when it was his anyway? Or at least, if not his, then not exclusively yours. You might call it marital property, even though you weren't ever actually married. Effectively, it was joint property. Anyway after you split up, the kettle seemed to stay with you. Till the day he came knocking at your door and said, "I've got the flu and all I want is a cup of tea. A bloody cup of goddamn tea, that's all I want. You know how to make tea—you know you can't boil the water for a proper cup of tea in a saucepan." "So I gave him the kettle," you said.

"Just like that? You just handed over the kettle, just like that!"

"No, no, that's just the beginning of the story. Pass me the octopus."

So I toss the octopus around a bit before letting go, let them slither and slide into a big white bowl. Splash some oil over them. Suddenly the pungency of olives is there, thick in the air. A pang of hunger, like a match igniting deep in the stomach. You squeeze a lime into the bowl and scoop up handfuls of the choppings, let them fall through your fingers, scarlet and green flashes. Put your hands in and mix it all up, swiftly, deft as a potter.

Now we pour some wine and roll some cigarettes. You can feel the warm redness filtering through your veins and the nicotine seeping like a long sigh through the length of your being. Taking time on our own terms, the time our dinner takes to marinate, we keep hunger at bay languorously, sipping, inhaling, continuing the story.

"No, no," you say, "I made him promise he'd give it back as soon as the flu went away. So after a couple of months, I asked for the kettle back—I felt I had to, to save face, otherwise he'd have it over me, the kettle." I imagine the kettle hanging in a doorway like a bunch of mistletoe and these two underneath, jammed there, locked in some indefinable and murky embrace. "One day," you say, "the kettle turns up on my doorstep with a big hole in it. I can't boil the water for my tea. After a few weeks, when I've calmed down, I call him up. First he says he never borrowed a kettle from me at all. I say, 'You must be joking.' Then he says, 'The kettle had a hole in it already when I got it from you.' I say, 'I don't believe this. Try the other leg.' He hangs up. A week later the phone rings. It's him and he says, 'I gave you back the kettle undamaged.'"

The gas is turned on and a match lit. A whir as the flame ignites. The octopus are tossed around once more and thrown on the griller. Green beans are steamed for a few minutes. Baked potatoes come out of the oven.

We eat, and you tell a story that began, in one version, in another country far away and very cold. "We were like orphans in the storm—exiles from a warm womb, Siamese twins curled around and entangled together. He'd go out in his sagging jacket with empty pockets and no money. I'd light the gas oven, open the door to let the heat into the kitchen, put on a record, put lentils in a pot to boil, chop onions till the tears would flow and stream. Streaming desolation as a guitar slides and a silky voice prowls through the house, every word insinuating menace: . . . *Ooh, isn't it nice* . . . Onions and menace, these are my domestic memories of those cold cold days, and a voice that strokes, that turns the chopping board to velvet—*when you find your heart*—a litany of drugs and suicide, of bored betrayal and petty accusation, but the words slither into oblivion; all you hear is the intonation, compulsively seductive—*is made out of ice*. . . . My kitchen lullaby. Then the door would open—cold air rushes in and he's there, large, shaggy, and roaring. With both hands he grabs his lapels, opens his jacket wide on both sides like a flasher or a gigantic benign bat. The inner pockets of his jacket are bulging: strange shapes and textures jostle mysteriously. On the laminex table he unloads the booty, throws his head back and laughs, a thunderous rumbling belly laugh. He's the Green Knight—when his head's sliced off, he picks it off the ground, holds it high for all to see, and laughs, a thunderous belly laugh that rumbles, reverberates through all the land. On the table he puts a tin of creamed lobster soup; French brie—squishy, redolent, and warm from snuggling by his heart; a paperback called *Do Androids Dream of Electric Sheep?*; a packet of oatmeal bannocks; a bottle of whiskey; an ancient book, elaborate gold lettering worn away, disappearing into greenness so that you can just decipher the title: *The Moonstone;* and two oranges—perfectly round, brilliantly orange."

We clear away the plates, scrape leftover octopus scraps into the bin, and now you open the cardboard box that has been sitting like a cat on the mat all through the meal. It's a very chocolate cake from the Kosher Cake Shop. In the neighborhood there are restaurants with names like Rusky Trattoria, Specialist Bistro, Froggies and Woggies, Thai Foon, Ping On, and the Disconsolate Trout. But there's one basic menu—on the first page there are pizzas, on the last there's Asian, and in the middle there are house specialties, which include dishes like chicken Kiev, creamed spinach, beef stroganoff. For dessert there are ten flavors of gelato and chocolate kosher cake. Where we go—on a big night out—

depends on what we want. Sometimes it's the ritual—all the restaurants have pink tablecloths, but only one, Froggies and Woggies, has folded deep rose damask napkins in the wine glasses. When you sit down, they welcome you and ceremoniously replace the cloth with paper napkins, a paler shade of pink. Or sometimes it's free association that matters more than ritual. "Ping On," you say, my foreign friend, "it sounds like an old Australian practice, like: 'Shall we go to bed or shall we just ping on?'" The Disconsolate Trout has exactly the same spring rolls as the other restaurants but served on embossed plastic dishes shaped like little fish with extravagant tails. Here you tell me this story: you had an affair, and all seemed to be going well when unaccountably the man started slipping away—he wasn't there anymore, nothing was said. You laid low for a while so no one could see the bruises, the imprint of rejection. Then when you'd had enough, you went out to a party where you knew he'd be and you bumped into him, so to speak, and speech was unavoidable, so you said, "I thought I'd brazen it out." "What's that," he said, "braised trout?"

The chocolate cake is rich, dense, unfathomable. In a flash I imagine inhaling. The infusion of nicotine disperses the density, lightens the atmosphere. I hold the cake in my mouth, enjoying the way it changes texture, slowly dissolves and melts; and I anticipate the end of the meal—a cigarette.

And then, after *The Moonstone*, many years passed and you were in another country where it was hot and all falling apart. You no longer sat in the kitchen waiting for him to return with magical gifts, purloined books and festive food. "He would come home," you say, "and I wouldn't be there. I'd come home later and he'd have gone—to bed, to another house, to walk in the streets. The kitchen would be dark and empty but there would be faint signs of his return, the ritual revelation and emptying of pockets. First there was a tin of Heinz tomato soup—on the edge of the table, in a corner, precarious. And then another, and another, a phalanx of tins, unopened."

Eating the cake becomes difficult, the more that's consumed, the more there seems to be. I try to eat faster so as to finish eating and start smoking.

"So how does it end? Do the tins just multiply in your absence?"

"No," you say, "it happened this way: one day I'm sitting in the kitchen looking at these tins, imagining every one of them filled with condensed anxiety. Can't open them, can't move them, can't read them. Then the phone rings. It's the cop shop—they say he's been arrested. Shoplifting."

"That's ridiculous." I can't eat any more chocolate cake, it's making me feel ill. "He'd never been caught, all those years, he was an expert—how come he got caught?" I want a cigarette, I want to cancel out the superfluity of food.

"He was caught coming out of a hardware shop with a chain saw under his jacket. Of course I never saw what happened, but you can imagine the scene: he edges past the checkout girl, shuffling sideways 'cause there's this huge bulge he's nursing that slips and slithers lethally as he fumbles for coins to pay for a packet of nails. She, the checkout girl, looks suspiciously at his misshapen stomach, and he tosses the nails in the air—they spray in all directions like tiny bullets, ricocheting on the shiny floor and metallic shelving. He makes a run for it and the chain saw slips, thuds to the ground, and there's a hand on his arm. The game is up."

I light up, inhale deeply, and the incipient nausea starts to disappear; I breathe easy. "So, when you went down to the cop shop what happened?"

"I never went. I couldn't bear it, the pain of this spectacle. And I knew that even though he wanted me to look, he'd never forgive me for what I would witness there. It was better like this—a clean break, dramatic."

"So that's the end of it? You never saw him again?"

"Well, no—yes, I saw him again—you know I see him now and then, just to swap books, recipes, sometimes I borrow his vacuum cleaner, sometimes he borrows my kettle. Nothing complicated."

The coffee's ready, and we pour it thick and dark brown into white cups. Drink it with a last cigarette. A perfect end to the meal.

I DONE

A LOTTA BAD THINGS

∞

Your enemy appeared just like smoke and, just like smoke, can be blown hither and thither.   ELIAS CANETTI, *The Agony of Flies*

There are times when you trip, and you don't know why. You're striding along when all of a sudden you miss a beat, lose the rhythm, fall in a flash on your face. And your face keeps falling, falling away from your body, tumbling away into a big black hole.

There are times when your whole body stumbles and falls into gloom. Into loneliness. Everyone recedes, friends shrink from you, lose their shape, regroup in swarms of animosity. Love reveals itself as fraud. You remember: smiles that were held a fraction too long, raised eyebrows, smirks, a caress that swerved at the last moment. You understand at last the intricate evasions, scarcely concealed gestures of contempt, malicious signs of mockery passed behind your back.

You seek refuge from persecution by locking the doors, unplugging the phone, drawing all the blinds to make the house dark. You turn the Living Room into the Smoking Room, and there you sit in the dark and drink scotch slowly and smoke one cigarette after another. You remember, and imagine. You rehearse retorts, execute finely crafted acts of vengeance, orchestrate dramas of reversal, and blow your enemies, just like smoke, hither and thither.

The room grows blacker and blacker as you smoke more and more cigarettes and feel sicker and sicker. And then, just as the blue tendrils of smoke snake through the foggy atmosphere and disperse, dissolving into nothingness, so the sociality of your venom evaporates. You turn on yourself. Why me? you ask. What have I done to deserve such cruel calumny? But even as you ask yourself this question, you can hear the reply. You hear Robert De Niro (being Jake LaMotta) answer: "I done a lotta bad things, Joey. Maybe it's coming back to me."

Then there is just blackness, a black pain in a space without time. There is only one thing between you and nothingness: smoke. You ingest cigarette after cigarette, until there comes a time when you notice the ashtrays overflowing with ash and the empty crumpled packs, and it occurs to you that time has passed and the cigarette supply is almost exhausted. Burrowing into the mire of melancholic masochism, you comfort yourself: ah well, if it all gets too bad, there's always a way out—I can always kill myself. Then, as you inhale this thought—feel it fill your lungs and filter through your nerves and arteries, and breathe it out as smoke—it registers in your being as, precisely, a thought. And you think, This is why Artaud thinks of suicide as an impossibility: because it involves a kind of voluntarism. The only kind of suicide that makes sense to him, he says, is "an *anterior state of suicide*, a suicide that would make us retrace our steps on the yonder side of existence rather than the side of death." He feels "no hunger for death": "I simply hunger *not to be*, never to have dropped into this sink of imbecilities, abdications, renunciations, and obtuse contacts."

This involuntary recall intimates, paradoxically, the possibility of a kind of cure through immersion. You might call it *smoking Artaud.*

You have smoked your way out of the black hole. Or, to look at it differently: You smoked your way into the black hole, and Artaud smoked you out.

THE SMOKING ROOM

∞

"Choose Not to Die!"

The words assaulted her, leaped out of the blurred newspaper print, destined for her alone. She was instantly receptive, alerted to the import of this personal message, coded and craftily transported through the most public of mediums. "Yes," she declared, struck by the novelty of this imperative, "it is, of course, a matter of choice. I can take my life into my own hands. Obviously." So she enrolled in a night class, lured by the promise that with a lot of dedication and a little training (six expensive lessons), she could renounce the insidious seduction of death.

The first lesson proceeded thus: the "subscribers" to the course (or "students," as invoked by the instructor—"You are students of life!") assembled in a circle in a small classroom, all perched awkwardly on hard plastic chairs. "This is the first lesson," said the teacher—or "leader," as he introduced himself, a florid and flamboyant man—"facing up to things, facing each other, looking into yourself." It was not a pretty sight. Forced to look around and meet the gaze of twenty or so other people, she saw an anomalous collection of souls united only in their shiftiness, their emphysema, and their gender. Most were women, though there were a few men who looked as though they were trying hard not be seen, or at least not to be seen as men. One by one, moving around the circle, they told their little tales of abject dependence, each offering a confession as a gift to the group.

Once solidarity was established, a contract entered into of mutual (and mutually supportive) commitment to life, all the doors and windows were ceremoniously closed by the florid man, who assured his captive audience that although he was highly qualified and had trained for many years to get where he was in a hard profession, in the end what guaranteed his high success rate was nothing less than personal experience. "The bottom line," he said, "is being there and doing it. You, Yourself, and No One Else." So, with all the doors and all the windows closed, all twenty people in the room sat poised with a cigarette and lighter in hand, and when he said, "Ready! Steady! Go!" twenty cigarettes were lit and smoked in unison, swiftly, deeply. Quickly the room filled with smoke—billowing, blinding, and acrid. People began coughing and groping for the door. But there was no escape. "Keep smoking!" the teacher commanded. "Quicker! Quicker! And another! Light up another!" She thought she would choke, suffocate, vomit, lose consciousness; yet despite all this, she followed his directions absolutely, obediently, sucking in smoke at a furious rate, drawing it deep down into her lungs, into her stomach. "Imagine your lungs!" he commanded. "Black. Filthy. Suffocating. Your lungs are like this room! This is your life!" At last the doors were unlocked, and twenty desperate bodies stumbled through the black smoke, tumbled out of the Smoking Room and into the cool night air.

Lying on her back on the grass, breathing serenely at last, and watching the clouds move wispily over the moon, she thinks of other smoking rooms. She thinks with identificatory pleasure of H. D. lying back on her couch, watching the smoke from Freud's cigar spiraling toward the ceiling, wafting wispily overhead. That would have been a better cure, she thinks, for whatever it is that ails me. She remembers Canetti's description of his Sephardic grandmother, who lolled magnificently all day and every day, never rising from her couch, smoking languorously and continuously.

The Smoking Room is traditionally a Men's Room—it is where the men retire together, escape from the ladies, and exchange lewd jokes and tall stories. Think of the mural *Men*

Without Women, painted by Stuart Davis in 1932 in the Men's Lounge at Radio City Music Hall. Or think of the opening of Molière's *Don Juan*. Sgnarelle is holding a tobacco pouch and says:

> Whatever Aristotle and all of philosophy might say, there is nothing to equal tobacco: it is the passion of gentlemen and whoever lives without tobacco does not deserve to live. Not only does it please and purify the human brain, but it also teaches the soul virtue and with it one learns to become an honest gentleman. Do you not see, as soon as a man takes some, how obligingly he acts with everyone and how delighted he is to give it away right and left wherever he may be? He does not even wait to be asked but anticipates people's wishes, because verily tobacco inspires feelings of honor and virtue in all those who take it.

A decade before *Men Without Women* Stuart Davis had painted a series of tobacco still lifes with titles such as *Cigarette Papers, Bull Durham, Lucky Strike,* and *Sweet Caporal*— paintings that fabulously combined a sense of the "thingness" of tobacco with a mode of cool pre-Warholian abstraction. As a smoker he was enamored of the accoutrements of smoking—the papers and pipes and pouches; as a painter immersed in modern American urban life, he was fascinated by tobacco as commodity and incorporated into his paintings the symbols, colors, and typography of tobacco advertising, of tobacco labeling and packaging. If smoking, for Davis, seems to have been equated with modernity, equally it was associated with maleness. He was particularly fond of, and featured in his paintings, a brand called "Stud" whose emblem was a rearing stallion. In the Radio City mural the stallion—alone this time, as a logo detached from the name—appears along with other elements signifying the realm of the masculine: a car and garage, gas pumps, barbershop pole, schooner, tobacco pouch, pipe.

Michel Serres identifies Don Juan as the quintessential ladies' man and as the first hero of modernity, and he also asks: "But would we ever have been able to read Molière without Mauss?" Eating, joking, smoking all constitute a circuit of exchange, a social contract. Derrida notes that in Molière it is a contract *between men*, just as it is in Mauss when he discusses the gift/sacrifice of the Winnebago (Sioux) chiefs, who put offerings of tobacco in the fire when welcoming their fellow chiefs from other tribes.

Tobacco may have been seen by men as the passion of gentlemen, but the Men's Room was traditionally seen by the ladies for what it was: a urinal. While tobacco figured, for writers like Molière and Baudelaire, as a sign of modernity, of modern urban life (albeit an older and more European version than Stuart Davis's), there was of course another insignia of the modern—inscribed not in a boys' pissing party but in a girls' salon. Smoking cigarettes in public became, for women, a significant sign of emancipation. Lola Montez caught this habit from George Sand and spread it around, just as in her turn George Sand was so impressed by Lola's getup (her dressing in black) that she copied the fashion and adopted it as her own.

Lying on the grass under the stars, she thinks of Gertrude relishing her cigar and her fame, and Alice orchestrating the soirees; and she thinks of *Prisoner,* the pleasure of settling back on the couch and watching the late-night reruns, of smoking in unison with the girls, entering a universe that revolves around the acquiring and hoarding of cigarettes, the dealing, the illicit gatherings, where they all smoke and ancient Lizzie coughs and they argue and joke and plan elaborate crimes.

The florid leader calls them to attention, summoning them back to life and back to the classroom. But she slips away, home to a room of her own.

K I N D N E S S

(or, the werewolf comes home)

∞

There comes a time when the ferocity of craving palls, you are drained dry by it, no longer do you want this savagery. What you want instead is kindness: searching for something other than the casual cruelty bred of addiction, you become fixated—all you can see in the world are signs and hints and subtle intimations of kindness. Walking in the street you're caught by a face, rushing to catch the bus you're arrested by a gesture that speaks kindness, in the cinema you see a man turn into a werewolf and you think of Labradors and golden retrievers and dogs for the blind, and you go soft in your center. Your need conjures into existence a gentle solicitous universe vibrating with good intentions that go forth and multiply—just as the magician conjures a rabbit out of a hat, and by this singular and miraculous act initiates a rabbitification of the world. When I contemplate your craving, I think of Brecht's account of the Temptation to Be Good, and I see that libidinal energy can attach itself even to kindness. I imagine you sucking the streets, gobbling all the trash and debris and detritus, just to find a speck of kindness, or sucking vampire-like all kindness from every living body, so that in the end there are only ghosts remaining in the streets—anemic ghosts, no longer wanting anything at all.

THOSE PLACES

IN THE BODY THAT HAVE

NO LANGUAGE EITHER

⌒⌒

Motionless, you're moving fast. For a day and a half you've been on the road, in the driver's seat: sitting still, you've been propelled through space, through differing landscapes, differing time zones. Around you the world has changed; inside everything is the same, except the music. It's the music that connects you to the world out there, pouring into the car through invisible speakers, bellowing out through the open windows, flooding the landscape. And something else connects you, though you only realize this when you stop as night falls, open the door, and put your feet on the ground. You feel suddenly charged with movement. The propulsion of the car and the rhythms of the music continue in your body, driving you forward into the night.

You are driving inland up the eastern side of the continent, through landscape that seems unmistakably Australian— scraggy pastures, small towns that could equally be large semideserted rural homesteads, occasional hilly outcrops— yet you're on a highway called the New England and passing through towns with names like Ben Lomond, Glencoe, Glen Innis, Emmaville, and Deepwater. The pastures around Deepwater are sad and dry, as though greenness had faded long ago, persisting in the dingy khaki as nothing more than a tired memory. Perhaps the name signals a misplaced hope in those early colonists, a hope that somewhere under the ground there were hidden rivers that one day would be divined and spring forth, turning the scrub into verdant English pasture, the knobbly hills into mountains of European grandeur.

Slowing down to pass through Deepwater, the country-and-western station on the radio starts to crackle and fade. You fumble in the box of jumbled tapes and pop one randomly into the player. Operatic voices fill the car, and a sense of elation almost lifts you from your seat. You turn the volume up, the voices swell, the roof quivers. You open the windows wide, and as you whip past a paddock of mangy horses, a wild whinnying fills the air: they are transfigured; like you, gloriously infected by *Rigoletto*. You breathe the music in, inhale the smell of it. It is the smell of leather. And with the smell comes a sensuous memory—of rhythmical rubbing, of dubbin, the pliancy of soft saddlery. You twitch your nostrils, sensing something more, another smell that rises with the voices, that mingles with the leather and circles through the car in smoky blue rings. It is the dense blue smell of Gauloises.

On the farm in Africa, when she was a child, there was a Sunday ritual, a rather haphazard ritual since it didn't occur with rigorous regularity, but when they decided to do it, it was done with ceremony. They would assemble a trestle table on the long low front veranda in front of the dogs' beds, and they'd drag all the saddles and bridles and halters onto the table and undo the buckles until all the tack was in bits and pieces. They'd put their bathing costumes on, fill buckets with warm water, and in a row on the table would lay out sponges and rags and Brasso and Silvo and bars of saddle soap and tins of dubbin. Then her father would open up the doors of the record player, take out one of the records, very carefully place it on the turntable, draw back the arm, and lower the needle, ever so delicately, so that it didn't scratch. The sounds of *Rigoletto* would flood the house.

The equine smells, the dirt and sweat rising through white suds, chocolate brownness seeping into the frothy creamlike surface like a storm in a teacup (or a perfect cappuccino, she thinks now). They'd wipe away the suds, gently dry the leather, and then would occur a moment of sanctity—the opening of the dubbin tin. Ceremoniously, dubbin would be applied to the leather and then the slow rubbing and polishing would begin, and the sublime smell would slowly seep out and infiltrate the sounds of *Rigoletto*. When it came to an end and both sides had played (a condensed version of the opera, the highlights arranged to fit on one LP), they would turn it back to the first side and begin again. The high point always was the famous duet, though it was not exactly the sublimity of the voices nor the exquisite tragedy traced in the lyrics that moved them, since they had no idea what the opera was about. Their delicious anticipation of this high point was dedicated to the performance of Shumba, the mighty ridgeback named for the lion he resembled. Every time and perfectly on cue, when Gilda's voice mingled with her father's, Shumba would lift his snout to the sky—moved either by ecstasy or unbearable audial irritation—and start howling.

Later she would wonder how *Rigoletto* found its way into that farmhouse in Africa, how it came so lovingly into her father's hands. Certainly he would never have set foot in an opera house, and although the record cabinet had been chosen (for its oak veneer surface) and installed with much deliberation and pride, it functioned more as a piece of furniture than as a player of music. She only remembers one other record from that time, the one her little brother, who was just mastering the art of this newly discovered technology, would play over and over again, for hours on end. First, there was "The Yellow Rose of Texas," and then he'd turn it over and on the other side was "Oh, Bernadine." Then back again— "but the yellow rose of Texas is the only girl for me"—and then again, that lovesick invocation "Oh, Bernadine," repeated with the same anguished groan, the same stomach-lurching cadence. Those songs must have faded from the universe, for she has scarcely ever heard them again, but sometimes something sets her off and she is in the grip of that old invincible repetition. Once she was in a cinema, deeply and deliciously immersed in the film, transported to another era, a universe of tremulous and attenuated emotions. The hero entered a florist shop: you could feel the dampness of the shop, sense the smells, and you could feel his desire careening, in a New York society sort of way, off course. He chose, as always, lily of the valley for his betrothed, but for the other woman he chose a bunch of fulsome yellow roses. Instantly, as the roses materialized on the screen, the soundtrack of the film was overlaid by a virtual presence, by a cowboy's voice intoning, "And the yellow rose of Texas is the only girl for me"; the words of the song, from beginning to end, played through her head, through the auditorium. And then began again. She felt, just as she had as a child, the lyrics and the musical notes driving, like nails, into her skull. Tortured, like Artaud, by a vicious god hammering nails through her flesh, into her bones. She was tempted to respond like Artaud himself, to hurl invective at the screen. But instead she closed her eyes, breathed deeply, invoked some residual shamanic power, and summoned into her being the sonority of *Rigoletto*, so that eventually the Texas Rose was vanquished and she could return to the film, exhausted, but receptive again.

She never learned the words of *Rigoletto*—they were, after all, foreign, in another tongue. And she never knew what it was about. Only much later, as an adult, when she went with a new lover to the Sydney Opera House to see a performance of *Rigoletto*, did the words sink in. Though even then it was more a replaying of earlier experiences that overwhelmed her. But afterward, smoking a Gauloise in bed, he told her the story, the story of a father and daughter, and recited some of the lyrics, and she tried to convey to him how *Rigoletto* smelled of horses and leather. He read to her from a book, about how sometimes the operatic "detaches itself from statements, disturbs and interferes with syntax, and wounds or pleasures, in the audience, those places in the body that have no language either."

It had been a passionate affair. An unlikely and fleeting liaison, it had flared like a redhead and just as swiftly burned itself out. You could also say, though, that it had gone on forever. Long ago she'd met him, in a steamy club where almost-naked beauteous beings writhed enticingly though with narcissistic relish behind bars on raised platforms, and Patti Smith and the Police boomed out from speakers that covered the walls from floor to ceiling, blocking out the world, erasing day and night. For weeks they lived in the dark, in sweaty places, in smoke-shrouded beds, in murky clubs, in steamy operas; and all the time she was wet and coming and coming again. Then it was over. He charged her with soullessness. It's true she didn't exactly love him, not in the kind of amorous way he seemed suddenly—revealing an entirely unsuspected Gothic streak—to want. But she did love being with him, she relished him and cherished him and wanted more. For a while she was grief stricken, or rather devastated by a painful yawning howl that rose up from her cunt and spread to the surface of her being, appearing in red splotches on her face and fingertips—signs of retribution displayed for all to see. Then the howling subsided, succeeded by a bout of petulance. The petulance was restorative and soon she was OK again.

A year later she bumped into him on the street, and they went for a coffee and told stories of their lives now. They laughed a lot and commiserated and empathized with each other's dilemmas, caught up as they both were in claustrophobically domestic scenarios. They began to see each other now and then: they would go occasionally to the opera; they would walk through the city and ruminate about the country, about the land and land rights and legislation; they'd swap books, talk for a long time on the phone, smoke on the phone. Sometimes they slept together, and it was always comforting, though never again was there quite that wild intensity of the first few weeks, of the passionate affair.

Over the years they came and went, only sometimes coinciding, but if the opportunity and money were there, they'd go together to the opera house in the harbor, or they'd beg or borrow a new CD of *Rigoletto* and play it and smoke Gauloises and inhale a leathery pungency. Then a few years ago a postcard arrived from over the seas. It was a reproduction of a painting, a very American painting of a winter scene: people—archaic turn-of-the-century-looking people—skating on ice, whirling, and promenading in boots and fur-lined capes and muffs in the snow. They are dressed in bright primary colors, but over everything is an icy blue patina; a palpable blueness rises up out of the snow and emanates out of the postcard, which lies on a table on a sunny pavement café at Bondi Beach. He writes, she reads:

> Am sitting inside, barricaded away from the freezing cold and searing winds. When I saw this painting yesterday, the blueness of it grabbed me—it's an icy cold blueness, but it's also the warm blue of Gauloise smoke. So I went out and bought a pack, for old times and for protection against this alien place. It is warm and delicious in here—smoking, listening to *Rigoletto*, the room is filled with the smell of leather.

Driving through New England, the car and the landscape are filled with music, with the smell of leather and the smell of Gauloises, with an indissoluble braiding of memories and sensations. Ruminating on sensate memory, on the way it builds in slow accretions, mapping a minutely shifting landscape, she ponders the peculiarities of love and friendship. What she can't figure out is why or how certain bodily memories persist, often charged by an erotic presence, but sometimes not. What is it that configures certain relations as charged—your relation to cigarettes, to a person, or to something else less concrete and definable, like place or childhood, say? Is it the always-wanting that fuels memory here: wanting more than you've got, wanting what you haven't got, wanting what you've lost? And how, she wonders, does this sort of dynamic relate to that other sort, where desire is somehow decathected, where the charge has been withdrawn from memory or transformed? Why is that some relations, even though they end (because the erotic charge could not survive quotidian immanence) do not go away—"they" remember you, and other relations never end but survive a transition from passionate intensity to something else, call it empathy or friendship? Here memories migrate—like cigarettes, they are shared; and after burning, the smoke lingers, meanders through bodies and landscapes, from a farm in Africa to the Sydney Opera House, from blue ice to khaki bush.

Deepwater is far behind her now; she is heading into high country that is lush and where the air is rare, and *Rigoletto* is coming to its tortuous end. As always she weeps as Rigoletto discovers that he has brought about the death of his own daughter, as those familiar phrases collide, as *Padre mio!* and *Mia figlia! Dio! Mia figlia!* become fatally and forever entangled. There is a pause, then the tape pops out and the local radio station reigns again supreme—it's Madonna and, as fate would have it, she's singing "Papa Don't Preach."

She's off on a new journey.

ANTICIPATION

(a crevice opening up)

∽

Opiates. The ineffable euphoria of morphine, pethadine. If you're a heavy smoker, then you don't risk your life with anesthetics. It's touch-and-go: going under. Terrified you lie there, imagining the end, seeing yourself a corpse. Scared stiff forever. Yet at the very same instant—between here and there—anticipating the pleasure of a premed hit. That flooding sensation and then a floating, delicious floating free . . . A fear of pain, of the wound, yet willing to endure it for the sake of a morphine high.

If it weren't for needles, I could imagine myself hooked on heroin. And I can imagine the crevice opened up by the desire for *neige*, for snow that filters memory, falls, and covers over the cracks. But imagine too the wound that's opened up when there's no satisfaction, just a perpetuation and intensification of desire, so that desire and need are folded into each other, miragistic.

"Just imagine!" they say, the caring professions. "There are those worse off." I *can* imagine. Every hour is spent imagining. This, the crevice opening up, is what I experience now in craving nicotine. But nicotine dependence has been culturally stripped of drama, puritanized, belittled. I need to reinsert it in a melodramatic scenario. For all of us who are rebuked, exhorted to act our age and behave like civilized adults, for us I want to shout and weep and berate the world, reclaim the stage, reclaim the right to histrionics.

HABIT

∞

It's hard to break a habit. Everyone knows this, and everyone knows that this is because drugs invade the body, filter through veins and arteries, jump synapses, simulate the flow of blood. So that in the end, or after no time at all, you're hooked.

"But everyone, as it turns out, is wrong," says Maggie. We are driving fast, careening over the Bay Bridge, away from the bright lights of San Francisco; and we are high on disaster. It's been a day of spectacular deaths—we've watched the waters of the world engulf Brünnhilde and we've seen Richard Gere propelled through space, betrayed as we knew he would be, yet again. The actual substances, Maggie tells me, aren't the problem. They can be got out of the body fast, detoxification is a cinch. In fact, so-called "illegal substances" are in and of themselves more often than not pretty insubstantial. The problem is memory. Memory is really substantial, a serious matter. She knows this because she saw a program on TV about addiction showing that there's a biological basis to the process, but it's not, as everyone thinks, based in the substance, in some inherent property of nicotine or heroin or Valium or alcohol or whatever. They said, on this program, that it's important for addicts to avoid situations associated with the substance, for it is this that provokes memory and memory is a killer. The way they described it is this: it's as though the memory (of pleasure, of gratification) is *burned* into the brain, it's there as a physical scar, indelible. The slightest association reactivates the scar, turns it again into a wound that craves healing. All you have to do is tease the surface.

We argue about memory and biology, but secretly I'm

taken by this image: by the physicality of memory being burned into the brain. It makes of the brain something very fleshy and gives memory a searing force.

Not long after this exchange with Maggie, I find myself again careening over the Bay Bridge late at night after a party, this time with a journalist who's doing a story about renunciation and the singles scene. All over San Francisco there are groups you can join, anonymously, to give something up and find someone new. The idea is intriguing: for a moment I'm tempted—at least you'd know from the outset that you had something in common. I say good night to the journalist and go home, to grieve alone in the hope that it will all soon pass.

A week later I find myself riding BART with a friend of a friend, who tells me how she kept falling in love with alcoholics and how she'd seen this program on TV that had made her realize it was *she* who was the addict, since it was the memory of her father drinking when she was a baby, a memory burned into her brain, that drove her to repeat this suicidal passion. She said she'd taped this program and watched it over and over again, and now her life was ruined and she never wanted to see it again. This tale of retribution summons up an image of the Woman Who Worries about Everything pronouncing: "People who write self-help books deserve to be torn limb from limb by wolves." By now I'd figured out that it must be the same program Maggie had seen, and so I asked her if I could have a look before she wiped these images from the face of the earth. So that's how I got to finally watch the program.

I looked over and over again, rewound and fast-forwarded, but there was nothing to *show* memory *burning* into the mind. There was some passing mention of repetition, but this image that Maggie brought so vividly to life, that I had anticipated with such relish, it simply wasn't there. She'd remembered wrong, or perhaps the failure of memory was mine.

Either way, an errant trail had been burned through the San Francisco night.

PANIC

The dream spreads like a stain: india ink spilled onto a sheet of creamy paper. On the paper a few glimmering words are written. Only a few, but they are words filled with promise—the beginning of a story. The black stain spreads, fills the frame, eats the words.

My dream is this: that you are dead.

I wake sobbing, unable to bear the brilliance of light, longing for the black of oblivion.

Grief and panic sometimes conflate. A thought of the future without cigarettes can induce terrible panic. It's like when someone dies, rejects you, leaves—you can't imagine living from day to day without them. Anticipating grief and loss, the body goes almost into spasm. You black out.

A SLEEPING PROBLEM

∞

She can't sleep. She's been awake for days on end, awake through nights that last forever. All she wants is to sleep. Standing at the window, looking out on an alleyway heaped with garbage, where a young emaciated woman with a big black muscular dog sifts through the refuse, she imagines closing her eyes and wafting away, down the yellow brick road into velveteen oblivion, and waking up to find herself standing at a window looking out on this city of everyone's dreams and seeing what everyone sees: a postcard panorama, the Empire State Building, the Chrysler Building, Forty-second Street, the world.

For years she'd dreamed of this city, of being here. She'd imagined an atmosphere electrified, where all you had to do was keep moving, keep breathing, and you'd be propelled into the future. Now she's here. Drained, exhausted, driven by some demonic impulse to pace this grimy loft, back and forth, or sometimes to emerge into the street and walk restlessly in circles. Over and over again she'd find herself pressed up against the glassfront of the local diner, using all her energy to peer inside and read the menu. Sometimes she'd open the door, go in, and sit at a window table, watch the ebb and flow of desolation in the street. Often there'd be scarcely any signs of life, and other times there'd be men in business suits milling hungrily. She was losing track of time but still had a tentative grip on space. This was New York and she was on the edge of the financial district and knew she should find comfort in this, should lie back and let the emanations of power ripple over her. Nestled in the benign shadow of an advantageous deficit, a girl should feel secure and sleep easy.

Mostly, though, it felt like she was on the edge of the world and the zombies in their pinstriped suits were getting closer: soon they'd arrive and break into the diner, hungry for human flesh. But then, out on the street again, wanting more than anything to lie down and sleep yet terrified of the torturing demons of insomnia, she'd prowl vacantly in the grip of something inhuman, and it dawned on her that this was it—the night of the living dead. This is it, she thought, and I am one of them, one of the zombies.

For years she'd wanted to be here, and now she's here, alone, staying temporarily in a loft belonging to someone she does not know, will probably never meet. She doesn't want to be here. Without him she can't eat, can't sleep, can barely talk. It's the middle of the day in the middle of the week and this is New York. She should be walking in the city but is too exhausted to make the effort; her body is stretched out, strung between time zones, craving sleep, craving his hand on her belly, him being there curled around her. She lies on the bed and closes her eyes and is wide awake.

She closes her eyes and imagines. This might work, she thinks. This might put her to sleep—if she lies there and imagines herself walking in the city, she might be captivated by the journey, enraptured by the dreamlike images, seduced into sleep. So she imagines: opening her door, going down the stairs and onto the street and walking to the edge of Manhattan—there the ferry is waiting to take her to Staten Island, and as the ferry glides somnolently over the water, she gazes for the first time at the Statue of Liberty. This cruising, it's like a lullaby, familiar, been here before over and over again. Or she imagines: walking in the other direction for a few blocks and taking an elevator to the top of the World Trade Center, there to enact the ritual she's heard about. At the top she turns her back on the city and faces inward, finds herself staring at a massive wall painting—bright acrylic colors and shapes that allude to some primitive genre preoccupied with origins and the arcane minutiae of hunting and gathering.

She walks around the periphery, gazing at the succession of murals, caught up in a trajectory of investment and accumulation and expectation. In the beginning there are stunted dark-skinned people, dwarfs or pygmies, and it looks as though they are shaking hands while a couple of cattle and a woman stand by. Then there are machines for manufacturing coins that stand in orderly piles. And then there are depictions in the naive style of computer-generated messages about stocks and shares and the day's trading. Here is the history of money—"The Lascaux Caves of modernity" is the phrase she'd overheard at Kalgoorlie, a mining town in the barren waste of Western Australia, where she'd been looking at a display on a pinboard in the old museum. "You should go to New York," she'd heard this voice say, a European accent redolent of history and culture and knowledge. "There in New York, at the top of the World Trade Center, are the Lascaux Caves of modernity." "Caves," the old bloke minding the display had replied, "don't need to tell us about caves. This is down under, mate."

THE SPECTACLE of money failed to put her to sleep. It made her hungry. She closed her eyes and imagined his tongue moving over her thigh, moving in circles, closer and closer. She hoped for the sensation that would make her forget he wasn't here, the delirium that would lure her into sleep. But it only made her remember, and she was left high and dry, wanting. Awake.

To sleep she needs to be wrapped around another body. Or to be in the cinema. Sometimes, curled into her seat in the darkness of the cinema, sitting close to the front, the images would float free from the screen and wrap around her. Remembering this, she gets up from the bed and puts on her shoes. She will brave the streets, walk until she finds a cinema, and when she does, she will go in and watch whatever is playing.

The power, the immensity of these images, this desert landscape, stretches her eyelids and she feels it burn her retina—the image is at once out there on the screen, stretching past the edges of her vision; and here, within, integral to her eye. A woman tenderly caresses a man's coat before she hands it to him. He is leaving again. In her seat in the theater, she feels the rough texture of his coat against her cheek. For a moment her eyelids close. A flutter, the action of closing, the movement lasts an eternity. She's sinking, a drug is seeping languorously through her lids. Resisting closure, she feels the stirring of a somnolent desire, the desire to submit to narcosis. On the threshold: between there and here, images on the screen and shapes and colors burning through her body. Then for a moment she gives in. As her eyelids close, the images merge; she dissolves in the turbulence of a kaleidoscope. As they ride away, the old familiar refrain echoes through her—*"That'll be the day"*—and as her body swirls into eddies, the phrase spins and recomposes rhythmically: *"That'll be the day, when you say good-bye, that'll be the day, when you make me cry."*

The red and green of the Indian blanket disperses, there's a struggle, someone's crying. They're at the airport, about to say good-bye, not looking at each other. She's leaving for New York. A woman with green eyes starts going up the escalator holding a little girl with red plaits by the hand. Suddenly the child with red plaits breaks away, runs back toward us, pursued by the woman with green eyes. They struggle. Then, unaccountably, postures of hostility are abandoned, shrugged off; they turn their backs on us, walk away casually, and ascend the escalator again. Suddenly the child with red plaits breaks away, runs back . . . They do this over and over again, ten times perhaps. Then without warning the struggle becomes vicious. All of us watching are aghast, frozen by the violence of this movement, this confrontation between woman and child—*"That'll be the day, you say you're gonna leave."* Then a voice shouts, "Cut!" Everyone sighs with relief, and the woman and child turn to each other and embrace. It's unnerving, this tenderness, emerging so abruptly out of violence; tears start streaming—*"You know it's a lie, 'cause that'll be the day that I die."*

She emerges from the cinema drowsy, surprised to find that it is daytime, that everyone is rushing, cars careening, jackhammers screeching. She walks slowly, head down, eyes focused on the pavement; she doesn't want to be susceptible to the stimulation of the streets—she'll just pretend it's the dead of night and nurse this sensation of sleepiness so that when she reaches the loft, she'll sink into bed and continue dreaming.

As she lies there trying to sleep hunger invades her, an insistent gnawing within. She drags herself off the bed, over to the other side of the loft, and opens a cupboard. There's a crush of cardboard boxes, crumpled plastic bags, a spillage of whole-wheat flour and brittle buckwheat noodles snapped into shards and dried herbs and brown flour. Accumulated desiccation. Nausea rushes into her body, like a javelin through the sky. Gut heaving, she lurches to the sink and throws herself over its edge. She anticipates relief, as though her body will involuntarily expel the toxins of insomnia. But all she can do is retch.

As the retching subsides, she finds herself staring at the plug hole: grimy, like the Rock of Ages permeated with grease and grayness. Her gaze wanders over the floor littered with used matches and scraps of screwed-up Juicy Fruit wrappers. One by one she lifts her feet and looks at her soles—black and mildly sticky. Like the stove. She sits in front of the typewriter and can barely discern the characters. She places the tips of her fingers on eight keys and presses down. When she lifts her fingers she reads, clearly: *asdfhjkl.* Something has been transferred from the machine to her hands. She stands in front of the bookshelves and finds she can't read the titles; a peripatetic mold has spread from the fridge, devouring letters randomly. All this filth has been attaching itself to her body, and her body has been transferring it into the sheets, and the sheets have been wrapping her in dirt. No wonder she can't sleep. She's been trying to dream in a garbage bag.

There are no cleaning products in the loft. She remembers when she was a child being taken to visit an old school friend of her mother's called Shasta. Her mother warned her beforehand: "Don't accept any food; say 'Thank you very much but I'm not hungry,' and I'll take you for a double brown cow at the Dairy Den as soon as we're through here. You see not everyone has to get married, and some people are quite happy that way, don't get me wrong, but they are a little . . . well, a little different—they have different standards from us." Shasta, as it turned out, *was* different and utterly exotic: she herself was festooned with shocking pink plastic jewelry, and her apartment was festooned with plastic plates in all colors of the rainbow on which all manner of exotic foods were congealed or flaking or moldering. There was no dining table and obviously she ate in whatever spot—on the floor, on top of the huge record player, in the bath—took her fancy at the time, and when she'd had enough to eat, she'd move on, leaving a trail behind her. The Stoics would have had a field day, being into the reading of entrails and signs of life in unlikely places. Shasta put her hand on her hip, looked her old school friend up and down, and declared very grandly, "My tolerance for filth is infinite."

There are no cleaning products in the loft. Galvanized into action by an intolerance that has grown with the years and been nurtured by encroaching insomnia, she rushes out to buy some Jif and Ajax and Lemon Fresh and disinfectant and sponges and steel wool. She has to fight her way through the streets, through a maze of plastic refuse, through crowds chewing on hot dogs and spitting venomous globules onto the sidewalk. She has to duck and dodge and run doubled over like a poisoned dwarf. At last she reaches the supermarket. As she wrenches open the door, familiar sounds welcome her—muted murmurs of enchantment mingling with music so reticent it hardly registers as music more like an indefinable but loving presence stroking the soul. Her body begins a dreamy dissolution, she feels she could waft through these aisles blindfolded and find her way to the shelves of Jif and Ajax and Lemon Fresh and disinfectant and sponges and steel wool, just as she rolls out of bed back home in her own bedroom and stumbles groggily but with absolute certainty to the dressing table, to blusher and mascara and eyedrops and *très très rouge* lipstick. In here in the supermarket the air is bright and people glide serenely, smiling without demand or expectation, sleep-waltzing with their pneumatic partners: shopping carts unctuously replete. As she is sucked tenderly into this palace of the past and future, she slips by others on their way out. They all clutch white plastic bags of various sizes, emblazoned with a red heart and a legend in Gothic script: *Thank you. I love you.* She pauses before the display of dog food and insecticides, reads aloud the labels on all twenty-three brands of kitty litter, chanting below her breath, the accumulated recognition working like a litany. Sleepiness is creeping into her. Past a multitude of cereals and comfortingly reminiscent hair products for highly damaged hair, she slithers, past the cans and cans and cans of tomato soup, past a shelf of alluring self-frosted desserts and painkillers packaged with utopic enticement. By the time she reaches the household cleaners, she is spiraling slowly downward, weighted by lethargy, almost dreaming. There, before a vision of conglomerate cleanliness, she sways, lulled by the colors of ablution: jade, deep lupine, blue sapphire, aquamarine, astral blue, mint, moss green, light cerulean, and deep eucalyptus. Just as she is sliding into oblivion, a voice jars her awake. "Stuff your museums, man, like the dude in the ad says, this here's your real interactive gallery." As she opens her eyes, they focus on an arresting new product; a neat packable box she has never seen before commands her attention. It reads:

ABLOOT HANDY DISPOSABLE GLOVES
5 assorted colors
Protects hands from icky, sticky, yucky, iffy, gooey, pooey things.
Fits either hand
Fits ladies' hands up to size 9
Handy, made in Taiwan for
Abloot International, El Salvador

She reaches out, her fingers quivering with desirous anticipation, but just as they are about to close around her quarry,
the words detach themselves from the box and swing before
her eyes like a hypnotist's pendulum—*icky sticky yucky, iffy
gooey pooey, ickystickyyucky, iffygooeypooey, ickystickyyuckyiffygooey
pooey, ickyickyickeeickeeeickeeeeickeeeeeickeeeeee . . .*

Something hits her in the small of the back, a sharp stab of
pain. She opens her eyes and sees feet moving in slow-motion, shopping cart wheels turning like windmills against a
medieval sky. She looks up from where she is lying on the supermarket floor and sees a booted foot about to collide with
her chin. She turns her face quickly; the boot whizzes over
her head, smashing dead center into a pyramid display of
"New New New Environmentally Simpatico Ajax." The containers fly in all directions, exploding on impact so that white
nonabrasive powder whooshes into the air and floats down,
sprinkling everyone and everything in a dense mantle of purity. So much for turning the other cheek. In the midst of
wholesale spluttering and sneezing, someone starts whistling
"I'm dreaming of a white Christmas" and a truculent voice
intones, "Goddamn junkies treat this place like a fucking rest
home."

She arrives back at the loft and unpacks her acquisitions:
an imaginative variety of cleaning products, a pair of sheets,
and a frozen pizza. Fills a bucket with hot water, but not too
hot, not so hot that it will burn her skin. For she never did
reach the box of Abloot Handy Disposable Gloves, it seems
she will always only dream of them, always they will remain

just out of reach but reassuringly there—on the shelf in Manhattan, Paris, Berlin, Melbourne. With her bare hands, she single-mindedly scrapes, sprays, scrubs, rubs, wipes. She sprays the mirror and watches years of accumulated grime dissolve, and then, before her very eyes, the faintest impression of some indiscernible writing magically appears. Gently she rubs, blots away the froth, and then she reads: "To be happy is to be able to become aware of oneself without fright." Hours pass—it seems as though days and weeks pass—and at last the apartment is clean. There are new sheets 187 on the bed, the covers are turned back, and a refurbished newly polished book lies enticingly on the plumped-up pillows. The frozen pizza is popped into a pristine, glowing home-beautiful oven, and while it cooks, she runs a bath, anticipating the therapeutic sensation of warm water lapping over her body.

In bed she snuggles into the clean sheets, opens her book, and makes sure she can easily reach the bedside light so that when sleep creeps over her, she can reach out and switch it off without jerking herself awake. The book she has chosen is the one that sounded, from the blurb on the jacket, most like a thriller. This is what she likes best at bedtime—thrillers and detective fiction, since they more than any other stories can take your mind off everything else, take you elsewhere, and from there it's easy to slip asleep. But when she came to wipe away the dust and grime on the bookshelves, she discovered that there were no real detective novels in this loft. So she makes do with *A Severed Head*. After an hour or so she decides that this is not a soothing experience, so she gets out of bed and goes back to the bookshelves. All the books have been written by women, and there are enough to last a year or so, she calculates. This is comforting. It means she won't run out and can avoid one of the anxieties endemic to travel. Will I run out of tampons in the desert? What if the plane is grounded in Dubai for eight hours and I get to the end of *Taipei*? And, once upon a time, will my supply of cigarettes last? Her eyes fall upon *The Golden Notebook*, and this seems an appropriate choice since she associates Doris Lessing with bed, having once taken *Children of Violence* there and plowed through it with a bottle or two of scotch when she could no longer abide life in a cold country of gritted teeth. She is utterly enthralled by *The Golden Notebook*, captivated and sickened by her own immersion, complete complicity with all this threshing around in the personal. By the time she gets to the end, however, she feels like she's an entanglement of cold spaghetti. She needs a cigarette and a coffee very badly, even though she knows this will keep her awake. Still, now that she's started reading, she can't stop—like running downhill, the activity gains momentum. She gets out of bed to make coffee and while it's brewing, she assembles a pile of short story collections, and then she walks around the loft with coffee cup in one hand and book in the other reading out loud. She'd thought that the short story would be sparser, more focused than the feminine novel, so intricate in its imbrication of tragedy, but in fact she finds that almost every story is a concentrated concatenation of self-immolation, assault, emotional mutilation, betrayal, mediocre madness, suburban decay, suicidal desire, masochistic matrimony. By the time she is halfway through Joan Didion, she can no longer stand up; the room is swimming, and she feels like she's in the driving seat of a powerful car that's totally out of control. All she can do is hang on to the wheel. She collapses in a heap on the floor. Blacking out, immense relief washes over her—sleep at last. But the world is black only for a few seconds. As she topples over, her forehead smashes into a small but sharply angular marble bust of George Eliot, and she is instantly awake, in pain, and panicking about the blood that is dripping over Jane Austen and Jean Rhys.

She makes some more coffee and looks out the window to see if there might be any clue as to what time of day and what day of the week it is. But it's night and all she can see is the young emaciated woman with the big black muscular dog, still sifting through the refuse. She has read almost all the books, and now she can't stop—she's careening on endorphins, she's wearing the red shoes and has to read as though her life depended on it. She unearths a pile of Mills and Boon and a fat book called *Gyn/Ecology* hidden in a brown cardboard box under the sink and enjoys a brief interlude of serenity as she sails through Violet Winspear's sado-saccharine scenarios of male hysteria and the pathos of virility.

Eventually there is only one book left. *The Bell Jar.*

When she has finished reading this, she knows that she can't do without any longer. He's on the other side of the world, she's renounced tobacco, so only one option remains. She needs it fast, but how to get it in this strange and hostile city? For the last dozen books or so, she has been haunted by the image of a white coated doctor who has insinuated himself into a range of unlikely plots. He turns her stomach; she has no resources left to deal with his predictable concern for her emotional well-being, his undoubted conviction that she can take control of her own life by simply taking stock of the situation.

She remembers that she knows someone in New York, someone called Maggie. She calls her, tells her what she needs, and asks for help. Maggie says, "I'll see what I can do, call me back tomorrow." The next day Maggie says, "I've fixed it—we're going to meet him in Queens tomorrow." By tomorrow she's feeling very weird, but Maggie comes to meet her, and they go together across the water on buses and trains and on foot. At last they get to an old warehouse, where people are reading poetry and there are some photographs of magic lanterns and a sculpture show. "I'll make the connection," Maggie says, "but then you're on your own."

He's very tall, wears a huge army surplus overcoat, is called Joe, and says, "Hey! Glad to meet you." He suggests they take a look at the sculpture show. They pass a chiseled figure—all nose, contorted, disfigured. "Take this nose," he says. "What do you think of when you think noses?"

"Roses," she says.

He looks crestfallen, personally rebuffed.

"Inhaling," she tries, "exhaling."

"Wrong," he says. "What you think of is the man himself—Sigmund Freud's the man you think of."

"Of course," she says. "I forgot."

"That's OK." He puts his head on one side and looks at her, not without affection it seems, but as though he's rather bemused by her presence. "Forgetting's OK, forgetting, remembering—it's all the same, that's what the man says. Inhaling, exhaling, it's wrong, but wrong is sometimes not so wrong. Try sniffing. Now in 1895, if I'm not wrong—and occasionally I am, but to err is inspirational, occasionally—now in 1895 or thereabouts, he was getting his shit together, our man in Vienna. That's the very year, 1895 or thereabouts, when he started on about projection.

"Not a bad move, when you think about it—made the man a career. Not the big-time though, not Hollywood—you want to think about Hollywood, forget it—what we're talking here is modest ambition, your run-of-the-mill bargain-basement paranoia. Wouldn't you say?"

She nodded.

"Economy. Economy and cocaine. It doesn't add up in the case of Dr. Freud. He had a real bad attitude to cocaine, our friend Freud, a touch of the obsessive there; fond as I am, it has to be said. 'Economy'—couldn't help himself, just couldn't help himself, couldn't resist the subject. Always going on and on about economy, cathexes and economy. But when it comes to cocaine, what do you think about—you think about the man and you sure don't think moderation, but there you go, that's the man for you warts 'n' all. And what about you?"

She could see a huge slimy frog covered in scaly warts hovering in the air between them. She thought: I must kiss him; this is the secret, this is the price I have to pay, and then this nightmare will be over, no more waiting—the frog will turn into what I want.

"Me? No way. It's not cocaine I want."

He raised one eyebrow, an endearing gesture. The frog evaporated and there was simply a man watching her, quizzical, concerned.

"I just want . . . I don't want much, just . . . to sleep . . ."

He put a hand—perhaps protectively, perhaps with menacing intention—on her shoulder. "OK, now what we're gonna do is we're gonna go look at some sculpture and talk some more, get to know each other some, then when we know each other some, perhaps I can figure it out what you want."

"I know what I want."

"Sure you know what you want." He smiled at her, a smile that stretched from bland civility into a lopsided, conspiratorial grin. He put his hand behind her shoulder, guiding her toward the stairway. The pressure was ever so slight; perhaps it was reassuring, solicitous even. Then he added this: "Trust me."

They walked up to the next floor and into the sculpture show. For this she was not prepared. All her traveling and all her reading and all her eavesdropping had not prepared her for this. It was an exhibition of the insides of bodies. Worm-infested hearts, flatulent inflated livers, stomachs stretched like limousines, ulcerous intestines, brains mashed to the consistency of gray scrambled eggs. She supposed they were all composed of artificial matter, but it mattered not to her. Joe was unperturbed. He looked at her ashen face and asked, "Are you feeling homesick?"

"I feel desolate and sick."

"Ah yes," he said, "for an old passion."

"No," she said, "these bodies, they make me sick. I wish I could smoke."

"He fell off a bar stool and died, you know, the guy who wrote that, twenty-something; there's a logic to it, though, when you think about it, always a logic to dying—take Jimi Hendrix or Kurt Godel. Godel proves you can't prove nothing, and then he starves himself to death 'cause he's suspicious of all the food he's given to eat, and why not? Who's to say it hasn't been poisoned, how do you prove it? There's a logic to anorexia, that's what I say, and if you take that to a logical extreme—and that's what we're here for, to go to extremes— then you can't escape the fact that logic is essentially 100 percent anorexic. 'And I am desolate and sick of an old passion.' Well if you write a line like that, then you're bound to fall off a bar stool, aren't you? So it's an old love, is it, an old love that's under your skin?

"Take this heart, for instance." He crouched down, peering intently at a heart, vivid in its plasticity. Passing his hand over the glass case as though to caress the naked heart, he looked at her with tenderness, as though it were her heart he caressed. "What does it take to heal a broken heart?"

Without thinking she looks at the heart, behind glass, a fleshy contusion rendered in obsessive and bloodily repellent detail. She averts her eyes and tries to resist the sensation of being sucked empty. "Do we have to look at this stuff? Can't we just get on with it? I haven't got much time."

"This stuff, all this stuff"—and he gestures around the gallery as though it were his private castle—"is the stuff that dreams are made of. And that's what we're here for, you 'n' me, to figure out some dreamin'. You know this, there's a logic to dreams and there's a logic to dying, but it all takes time, no good rushing. Now take your average brain tumor. Who gets brain tumors? Intellectuals get brain tumors, that's who. And heart attacks? Well, if you're emotionally fucked up, you'll get a heart attack for Christmas. But insomniacs, now that's a difficult one—hey, man, take a look at this pancreas!" He stared at it for a moment with wonderment, and then he turned away from the glass cage and toward her, transferring his wonderment from the pancreas to her. "Tell me, what is it you want?"

"I just want to sleep."

"Some would say—not me, of course, far be it from me—but some, brave men who've trod the royal path to dreaming, some might say it isn't sleep you want. What you want is . . . just to want."

"Listen, I just want to break this habit, this not sleeping. Just give me a bit of something, whatever you've got, even a few pills if you've nothing else, just a few, something or other to break the habit."

"Tell me: I give you this stuff, then what happens?"

"I go to sleep. That's what I want."

"You sure about that? You just wanna sleep, that's all?"

"That's all."

"OK, OK, I get it."

Relief! The blood starts flowing back into her body, she imagines sleeping and waking up refreshed and being alive in Manhattan. She puts her hand out.

"Gotta think about this one," says Joe. "Leave it with me, leave your problem with me, go home, relax, hang out. We'll be in touch."

He takes her hand and shakes it, gallantly. Shambling away, he murmurs to himself, "I have been faithful to thee, Cynara, in not smoking."

Her friend Maggie says, "Trust him, he'll be in touch. I guess." The thought of the loft fills her with dread; she can't go back without a guarantee of sleep, so she moves, without thinking, in the wake of Maggie and her friends. In this city people sleep at odd hours, so there is always someone awake, always places to drift in and out of. People are kind. In a club a group of girls with spiky blond and pink hair and a large white rat come up to her and one of them says, "Gee, you're the Australian with the sleeping problem." "No," she says, "I'm not Australian, just lived there once for a while." In a bar where Andy Warhol used to hang out, a man in tortoiseshell glasses, who speaks in a deep seductive murmur, murmurs in her ear, "Tell me about your sleeping problem." Everyone wants to meet her. She is dimly aware that this might be the closest she ever gets to fame.

At last the message comes through. Maggie gives her the address where she is to go the next day at three o'clock in the afternoon. Joe will be moving some paintings. She is to stand on the corner of the street and look out for a pink van. When it pulls up and stops halfway down the street, she should count to a hundred and then make her way, inconspicuously, to the alley behind the street and walk slowly north.

So, just after 3 P.M. the next day, she finds herself in a claustrophobic alley walking in a direction that she hopes is north. The alley is deserted, nothing happens. Then an arm emerges from a doorway and beckons. She walks gingerly toward the doorway, standing well back to get a good look, to have space to split and run if needs be. A large shambling figure in an old army surplus overcoat steps out into the alleyway.

"Hey! Glad to meet you again," says Joe, shaking hands. He leads her into the doorway of what appears to be an abandoned building and pulls a crumpled brown paper bag out of his pocket. "What we have here," he says, cradling the bag in his large hands, "is some real stuff—this here's the real stuff, the stuff, between you and me, that dreams are made of. Well, I thought about it hard, you know, your problem, but, man, I couldn't get my head around it, then in the middle of the night it comes to me—dreams! That's what this girl needs: she needs some dreaming. What she wants—now that I can't supply. There ain't no substitute, no substance that'll fit the bill, no cure that's pure. But what we got here is the crème de la crème of narcosian cuisine. In this little brown bag is an experience to be savored, an experience, you might say, of a lifetime, a purple passage even." He opens the bag. "There isn't much to say or much to give—as you can see, the quantity is small but enough, enough for a single take that'll take you out, out there where dreams will melt the hardest habit." As he hands the packet over, he says, "Now promise me this: savor the taste, and take your time dreaming, take your time, slowly. Then later you'll remember and that's all you'll need, the memory, to imagine."

The brown paper bag has an old-fashioned feel to it, like a teddy bear; she holds it carefully, cradling it against her chest. "Thanks, I'll give it a whirl. How much will it be?"

OPEN ARMS

∞

A momentary memory, memory of a moment.

In that moment she does not know where or who she is. Bleeding from a gash on her forehead, she is standing in front of an old farmhouse surrounded by trees. The door opens, a man comes out, catches sight of her, throws his cigarette down, and opens his arms. "Oh, darling," he says, catching his breath, "come here."

The next moment segues into ordinary time. Crying, she is also being held close, she knows who she is, she knows she is home.

She is fifteen, it is Christmas day, and while riding in the *bundu* her horse puts his foot in a hole; as he falls, she flies right over his head, landing on her face. She remembers seeing the horse disappear into the distance, and she remembers registering both that she is bleeding and that this is the middle of nowhere, no dwellings in sight, only bush in every direction. After that there is a blank. Later when they reconstruct events, she realizes that half a day must have passed, hours lost to conscious memory, before that instant she remembers so vividly, that moment of disorientation—between remembering and forgetting, between having no sense of self and of being recognized and summoned back into the world.

Her father: three gestures, three movements temporalized, sequenced, each one vividly distinct and yet indistinguishable one from the other. He throws away his cigarette, he opens his arms, he hugs her close.

FIRE ESCAPE

∞

Why is it better to last than to burn?   ROLAND BARTHES, *A Lover's Discourse*

I enact fanaticism. Extrapolating every obsessive nuance from an arcane repertoire of bodybuilding gestures. Instead of smoking. In order to resist the memory, I meditate and stretch and walk a tightrope, never looking down, only straight ahead—into an old-age future full of graceful backbends and carrot juice insouciance. Still, I retain a skepticism about the "healthy body," about this mythically modernist corpus as generative of a "healthy mind." How can anyone with their wits about them possibly believe in a healthy mind? Yet a rampantly pernicious faith attaches to this ontological impossibility.

A healthy mind is like a body of writing in which all fury has risen to the surface and there been scrupulously skimmed away by the janitors of moderation. They who lurk with their nets and weights and balances, wads of blotting paper and fire extinguishers.

Robinson Crusoe recounts the advice given to him by his father. The father exhorts his son to persevere, not to deviate from the "middle station of life." It is a chillingly detailed passage of writing. The details are passed on, not merely down the line of inheritance, down the line of least resistance (on the contrary, as the younger son, Crusoe's inheritance is ambiguous), but into, and through, the body of this supremely narrative text. The paternal advice constitutes a speech that fathers fortune and inscribes a whole tradition of Anglo-Saxon morality. It is a speech about retention and the building of fire escapes. On "his" island Crusoe constructs a building with rooms to hold all his worldly goods, going to elaborate lengths to safeguard them against the weather, theft, and fire, while he himself continues to sleep in a cave. The exercise of self-denial is evident. But the contortions of virtue are more intricate than one might imagine. Through a characteristically Puritan mode of elision, the body is conflated with worldly goods. Through this procedure, the body is in fact objectified, distanced. It can only be kept safe if detached. It is put in a safe place—that is, not the sleeping place, not the bedroom. By this maneuver, the mind is protected from clutter—mind and body, separated out, are actually coerced into a negatively metaphrastic liaison. We can read *Robinson Crusoe* as a dual-purpose manual, to do with abstinence and building—bodybuilding, empire building, character building, and home building. It is the Anglo-Saxon mode of construction—you build the fire escape first.

It galls me to be renouncing nicotine now as the new moralism gathers and rises and suffocates. Every time I drive over the Horseshoe Bridge and see that video image of Yul Brynner, I want to throw up. There he is projected against the sky, larger than life, flanked by up-to-date statistics detailing the number of deaths in this state caused by smoking. Stop smoking, smell better, and live longer, they say. Be prepared! If you've got a clean mind in a healthy body, then come Judgment Day you'll make your fortune. You can fight your way to the front of the fire escape queue with a clean conscience. Don't squander matches, shore up against the future, invest in safety deposits. In the face of all this, the adolescent romance of smoking returns, seductively: an edge of seediness, tackiness, dingy saloons, the glamour of delinquency. To smoke is to break the rules, to affront, to refuse the compact of civility.

If there is a strain of romance that circulates through the sordid and the flamboyantly excessive, so too there is a romance of renunciation. Take *Casablanca*. *Casablanca* makes you feel good for simultaneously giving up and holding on.

It's the Puritan romance of anal retention. *Now, Voyager* is also about renunciation, I suppose, but at least it flirts with perversity, and it's profoundly acute in charting the ruinous relation between smoking and desire. Think, though, of those other movies, fraught with urgency, those that ask—and it's not an idle question—*Why is it better to last than to burn?* Think of *A Bout de Souffle*, *Written on the Wind* and *The Bad and the Beautiful*. (*Gone with the Wind*, though it is less about renunciation and all about romance, is nevertheless finally dedicated to a vision of *rebuilding*, of endurance. A pragmatic lesson arises out of the conflagration: in order to preserve the white colonial dream, build a fire escape first.) Think of Emmylou Harris—in the face of utter loss, of the irretrievable, she sings: *"And the prairie was on fire."* Here, it isn't even a question of which is better, but neither is there any question of escape, of calculated survival. He's burning in the desert and she's alive. So when she sings, *"I don't want to hear a sad story, full of heartbreak and desire,"* she means it, but nevertheless she must tell the story, register—in her voice—this incendiary sadism, this being-eaten-aliveness.

AGAINST THE tradition of *Robinson Crusoe* and *Casablanca*, there's a lineage undoubtedly romantic in its own way but less retentive—Brünnhilde, The Doors, Peggy Lee . . . When Peggy Lee sings *"Is that all there is?"* so much depends on "all." Or nothing.

၆

You are alone, on a deserted stage, facing a crowd. They
seem, all these people, to project hostility toward you. Or
perhaps it is merely indifference. Either way, they whisper to
one another and shuffle restlessly, laughing at each other's
jokes, ignoring your presence. Already on the stage, on public view, there is no way to back out of what it is you have to
do: deliver a lecture; so you take a deep breath and prepare to
begin. First you take out your papers, then a crumpled plastic pouch of tobacco, and then a box of matches—none of
which you have touched for a month. Ceremoniously you lay
out a paper. With one hand, you pull out a clump of tobacco,
dropping it into the palm of your other hand, teasing out the
strands between your fingers. Then you roll the tobacco gently, conjuring a cigarette shape, slim but not too tight. You
roll it just long enough to release that familiar narcotic scent,
at once acrid and sweet. It's a smell that reminds you of the
tobacco barns on the farm, the heat of the furnace, the leaves
withering and growing transparent. You drop the tobacco
into the paper, roll it deftly, lick and stick and twirl it between
your hands, and then you place it between your lips. You draw
yourself up, strike a match, and light up. Suddenly all eyes are
upon you; as you inhale deeply, the tip of your rolly flares, and
you feel in that moment that you are on fire, that *you* are a
flame licking through the crowd, drawing them all into your
orbit.

You begin; you say: "A month ago I gave up smoking . . ."

Canetti tells a tale of an arsonist, someone, that is, who
follows the urge to *become* fire. She begins as a young child
and spends many years in penitentiaries. She likes fire, but she

also likes confessing. When she starts a fire, people come to watch, and so when she confesses, she reconstitutes that scenario—people come to watch her, and she becomes the fire. "She must, early in her life, have experienced fire as a means of attracting people," writes Canetti. "She keeps it alive by suddenly transforming *herself* into the fire. This she achieves very simply: she confesses that she caused it."

U N S P O O L I N G

She turns a corner delighted by this scene of foreignness. The sound of Italian voices, rippling, cascading over the cobblestones, burbling through the chinks of silence as motorbikes are kicked, die, whir, and roar. She turns a corner.

And there he is, propped in the doorway, watching the scene, casual, drawing on a cigarette. Rushing around the corner, she is propelled toward a collision. Pulls herself up, the delight that has made her step light turns to tension. She finds herself frozen in the act of falling. Into his arms. He looks, doesn't smile. If he'd smiled she could have slapped him, wiped the smile off his face. He looks serious, relieved: she is here where he expects her to be, cascading round the corner.

After all this time, all the time it's taken to forget, he turns up again, far from home. All it takes is the turning of a corner to unspool, in furious fast-forward, all the work of forgetting.

He'd called her bluff, though was it bluff? she wondered later. When you act out last resorts, when you say or mutter or shriek out things you don't mean and utter words you didn't know you knew. One day she said, "Go away," and he'd turned his back on her and walked away. At first she could only see his back, could only experience the sense of him walking away, even though he was immobile, a figure suspended in space and time. She wanted, she willed, the distance—between her craving eyes and his recalcitrant body—to grow. But it didn't. Then slowly, with the passing of time, she begins to emerge from catatonia, starts shedding the pall of passivity. His back begins to waver and recede. She rages, and the back, a timid phantasm now, crumbles into ash.

She becomes articulate and writes a million letters that begin "You bastard . . ." Initially entranced by a mode of automatic writing, by the transference of passion and desire from the body to the page, she eventually becomes bored by the tedium of repetition.

She tears the letters up. She stops smoking. She stops writing.

She speculates on love. She believes that she has disentangled the imaginary and the conceptual, formulated a theoretical account that is profoundly innovative and acerbically accurate. She tells everyone, friends and family and her cat and strangers at the bus stop. "Hey, have you heard the one about love," she invariably begins. But they do not know how to listen. They lose the thread, get bored, mutter about referentiality and delusions.

She begins running. Early in the morning, secretly. It's a matter of getting through the pain—that point where your limbs are heavy and sinking, immalleable, implacable, you can't breathe, chest aches. You shift into automatic, plow on, endure. Then suddenly there's a change: a surge of euphoria, energy, there's a drug shooting through your veins, you're flying high.

She is amazed—she who has always scorned the pursuit of fitness—she is amazed at the revelation of such pleasure. She cultivates this vice, nurtures her secret, grows silky and lithe and enigmatic. She immerses her face in steam and rejoices as the impurities—the clogging, rancid residue of anachronistic desires—float free. In the mirror she wipes away all traces of a prior existence.

She reads books about running, and scours shop after shop for tracksuits and running shorts, and tries on shoes and more shoes, and ponders the modern miracle of choice.

In the library, filling her arms with books on running, her eye is pulled along the shelf. Whizzing through the alphabet, her gaze careens ineffably to *W*—WOMEN AND WEIGHTS. In a moment of acute insight, she is struck by the two *W*s or double-yous, by an arcane chain of doublings, an effacement of negativity, a refusal of absence. Imagining her body remodeled, herself in control, she takes up weights with a vengeance. Grows hard and lean, skin tingles.

Then one day she notices that nothing around her has changed. In the cat's red bowl there is kangaroo meat, and in its yellow bowl there are Whiskettes. Evidently it has not starved, nor pined away, nor suffered from sympathetic magic in her time of trauma. The pot plants have been watered. She feels suddenly and inexplicably better, purged of loss, free of renunciation's irritable myopia. But also, as she wakens into the world again, the compulsion of routine, the familiarity of the domestic, is disheartening. Through all this time it seems she has been getting up each day and going to work, although it has scarcely impinged on her consciousness. She claims all her accumulated leave and buys a round-the-world ticket.

First stop Italy: she turns a corner delighted by this scene of foreignness. The sound of different voices, rippling, cascading over the cobblestones, burbling through the chinks of silence as motorbikes are kicked, die, whir, and roar. She turns a corner and there he is, propped casually in a doorway, waiting, drawing on a cigarette.

In a café he spoons sugar into her espresso and then into his cappuccino. She stirs her cup, not really to dissolve the sugar, more to watch the creamy ripples; she holds her spoon up and watches the creamy brown liquid slide down over the shiny metallic surface and onto his tongue. He goes to the jukebox, leaving his pack of Gitanes on the table. His back to her, he leans over the machine, tossing a coin back and forth, and her gaze slides from his ass, blue-jeans tight, to the blue of the cigarette pack. The smoke seems to float free from the pack, to waft about her, whir across the room, and wrap around his body. *"You want me to act like we never kissed"*— Patsy sings, still singing here the same old song she's sung before, in the laundry sorting the whites from the colors, driving through the desert, dancing for no reason, just the two of them at home in the middle of the night. He returns to the table and starts telling her a story about his travels, but with that way he has, as though continuing a tale to which they've both been party, as though there's been a new and unexpected twist to events, a turn-up for the books. Holding his cup in one hand, he lifts the pack with his other and shakes two cigarettes loose. He puts one in his mouth and the other in hers. She takes it out and lays it down on the table. Shrugging quizzically, he lights his own, exhales with pleasure, and continues the story. For a long time she listens silently, distractedly, begrudgingly. Casually then, without realizing what she's doing, she picks up the cigarette and finds by holding it that she can calm her nerves. It's easier than she thought it'd be, to hold the cigarette and not be tempted, to feel indifferent. She starts enjoying the story, the familiarity of the drama. She lets the cigarette dangle unlit from the corner of her mouth. When he stubs out his third or fourth cigarette and reaches for a new one, she picks up the lighter, flips the flame, and passes it from the tip of his cigarette to the tip of hers.

Their smoke intermingles, circulates, as always, as though it always has.

DEMONS

∞

I wake in the night and the tread of their feet whispers in my brain. . . . I have
no peace for they are in me . . . in me. . . .   JACQUES TOURNEUR, *Cat People*
(1942)

It's the Cat People who haunt Irena. For me it's the Demons
of Nicotine. Before, I'd lie awake at night, body exhausted,
mind speedy and febrile, charged by stimulants. This kind of
insomnia was familiar—like the witch's cat, you lived with it
and read a lot of books while other people slept. Now I fall
asleep like a child; but it's false security. In the early hours of
the morning, I'll be suddenly shaken; as though physically assaulted, in an instant I'll be alert, wide awake. Sleep is ban-
ished. I wake craving and haunted. Is it the craving for nicotine that wakes me, or is it the dread—which then triggers off
a craving? The dread—both of smoking-again and of never-
smoking-again. Of course it may have nothing to do with
nicotine; it might just be a dread of being awake, and alone, in
the middle of the night. Like Irena, I'm caught between desire and terror . . . "they are in me"—the demons . . . in me
. . . This is what it feels like when I wake in the night.

   Irena finds her identification in that which terrifies her
most. She wants to be good, she wants to be loved, yet she desires something else: to be not her (apparent) self (a masquerading miss, heir-apparent to mr. middle-of-the-road-
america). Becoming the desirable other—this is an act of
irreducible destruction; it is an identity made manifest in fear
and loathing and exquisite satisfaction. So sardonic, this film,
and so unnerving. It's only in the cinema that you can get
these impossible conjunctions; you can't do it with words on

a page—you need to be in the dark. It's this that makes *Cat People* work—it keeps us away from the light. We don't know for sure which side we're on, whether the demons are out there or in here—not just in Irena, but ". . . in me . . . ," or in the stranger sitting next to you.

Identification and desire. These dynamics imbricate the smoker and the renunciating smoker. An identity you've grown accustomed to over twenty years. You'd think this would have been time enough to domesticate the demon, to pull its teeth, so it'd be easy to kick it, boot it out of the house, watch it rolling without resistance, tamely, into the street. But, no, it doesn't happen like that: when you kick it, you take a chance, like the illusion of Russian roulette—it might be yourself you're out to kill, and you might succeed.

∞

Waiting in the doctor's waiting room, anticipating a grue-some prognosis, she thinks: Should I make a will? Or is this to

tempt a mordant fate? Immediately she starts divesting her-self of things, bestowing gifts upon her friends: the car to X, the cat to Y, the VCR to Z, the TV to AB. It's not as difficult as she'd imagined it would be, there's a certain relief in strip-ping back. To be without the burden of a car—always break-ing down, accumulating parking fines, rusting away—this could be a kind of solace. Catless, she would never have to en-dure the trauma of another feline fatality. But bookless, that would be a different matter . . . Without her books she would be . . . bereft. Though if I'm not here, she reminds herself, then bereavement is someone else's business. Think of this, however: if I die without a will, what will happen to my books? They might be thrown away, or tossed in boxes and sent to some musty cellar, or delivered up as a sacrifice to family members, who would tip them into a big pile and burn them. Not potlatch exactly, though a kind of payback, deco-rous malice masquerading as cleanliness, a suburban purging. They see in books, my family, a tumorous propensity, and in my death they'll be confirmed—they'll see a link made man-ifest between the acquisition of books and the catching of cancer. By turning this unwanted gift (of the books) into an act (of burning), they would make of their act a socially useful thing—a gift to society. I must make a list immediately, she thinks, lots of lists, in fact. I must sort and catalog the books, put them in piles, and then they can be shared out among my friends. Each friend will get the kind of books appropriate to their being. This way too the books themselves will be gratified: they'll breathe and continue living even though I will be long dead and buried, and when they read my books, my friends, they'll breathe in the gratification and think of me with fondness and affection.

She finds a grubby used envelope (containing an unpaid bill) in her bag and starts a column on the back of it, a list of lists, an assemblage of categories, a speculative delineation of genres. On another grubby envelope (containing a rejection letter: your manuscript shows some signs of life, but not enough, alas, for us), she writes the names of all her friends, and some acquaintances, and lovers, and ex-lovers, and ex-friends, and people she'd like as lovers, and some she'd fancy as friends, and even, why not, some impossible objects of desire. In the process, a few difficulties arise—the categories tend to bleed and blur, and then there is a hydra-headed question: how to allocate the gifts, how to mesh and match the categories of books and persons? Perhaps it's better to dispense with conceptual divisions, to operate more intuitively, to be guided by the feel and shape and color and smell of books and people. She thinks of her beloved Charmaine Solomon, a large and comforting book, a book that you can cradle in your lap, a book that cradles you, whose lustrous colors nurture—the shiny purple black of eggplant and nori, the yellow ocher of turmeric and dark orange of saffron, the burnt brown of yellow-bean paste and the red of bird's-eye chilies. These are Fiona's colors, the colors she wears and the moods she emanates, and so she will leave this book to Fiona. She is pleased with the perfect fit, the ease of ascription. But then she imagines Fiona holding the book in her hands as though she has been lumbered with someone else's recalcitrant baby—a squalling baby, stinking of urine, sodden to the touch—and saying, accusingly: "Are you trying to tell me I'm a lousy cook; I need a cookbook!" No, no, sorting by colors won't do. She will give this book to someone who loves cooking—she'll give it to Belle. As she makes this decision, an image of Belle materializes, holding the book in her hands and saying, "So you're trying to tell me I'm not an intellectual, no good at thinking, only cooking!"

Thus she is in the waiting room waiting, drawing up categories, instituting boundaries, redrawing, reclassifying, shuffling, wishing she were at home with her word processor, where the task could be simplified, a paperless matter, a matter merely of highlighting, erasing, inserting, replacing. Instead here she is surreptitiously ripping pages out of the waiting room's magazines, surrounded by endless scraps of paper filled with lists and crossings-out and arrows that meander in contorted trajectories, often veering off the page. Thus she is waiting when suddenly the door from the doctor's room opens and a vaguely familiar figure sashays into the waiting room, exuding an air of triumphant reprieve. It is Maggie. Her triumph, like radiation, sears the atmosphere.

She has known Maggie, a singer and songwriter, for many years, though she scarcely sees her anymore, and never by choice. Once they knew each other well, but now they only collide awkwardly and accidentally, at the hairdresser's or the butcher's or the gym. Maggie is a neat, sunny, prim person who sings limpidly about enervating and moderately perverse passions, about self-mutilation, shooting-up, anorexia. She is commonly conceived of as a seeker after truth, much admired for her searing honesty and stylistic courage. She possesses, so the critical orthodoxy has it, a "startlingly original voice."

Not from where I sit, though, thinks the woman in the waiting room who's writing lists while she waits, not very original at all. Of course it's not as though she values or even believes in originality, but having had her words stolen, she's suspicious and cautious. Long ago she'd confided in Maggie: late into the night they'd talked, she smoking and drinking scotch and wailing, Maggie sipping chamomile tea and listening. Maggie knew everything about her illicit and tortured affair with a very visible public figure and was encouraging her to turn it into fiction. "You're addicted," Maggie had said, "possessed. And this is silly. You have to turn the tables, *you* must take possession, you must make it *your* story." She followed Maggie's advice, documented the affair with veracity, religiously recording all her abject experiences, attentive to every ignominious and humiliating detail. The only other person she confided in was her hairdresser. He, too, was a man of optimistic vision. When she'd first visited him in despair about her hair, which was limp and thin and resolutely nondescript, he'd said, "Radical change is conceivable. Think of your head as a landscape: anything is possible." One day they'd been engrossed in a complicated coloring job, involving a lot of tin foil and layers, and in the background had been a New Age radio program on faith, selfhood, and otherness— occasionally some sound bite would float to the surface, and they'd laugh, enjoying the inanity. Then they heard a voice say, a voice coming from the wilderness: "We are not born to be free; we are born to be possessed." "There you go," said Peter. "It's a title for your novel: *Born to Be Possessed.*" She was jubilant; with this title under her belt, she felt it all fall into place, the massive accumulation of meaningless experience, the miasma of diaristic tedium. With this title, she felt she could at last aspire to fiction, escape the stranglehold of real-life experience, the gentle tyranny exuded by the No-Nonsense Melbourne School of Mediocrity. She told Maggie about this gift that had fallen her way, and they celebrated. A year later, the night before Maggie's first novel was due to appear in print, they celebrated again. "Let's drink now," said Maggie, raising her glass of champagne, "to friendship."

The next day Maggie's new album appeared: *Born to Be Possessed.* Treacherous, untruthful, hyperbolic, and derivative, it was nevertheless almost universally applauded as an ingeniously courageous act of lyrical veracity. When confronted she'd said, "No one owns words. It's not we—you or me, to be precise—who speak language; language speaks us. We are ready already possessed."

Now, some years later, they are in the doctor's waiting room. Surrounded by diagrams of blackened lungs and cancerous cervixes and once-elegant bones now mangled by osteoporosis, they talk nervously of death, of their own narrow escapes, of friends who've met unexpectedly sticky ends. Maggie says, "Do you still smoke?"

"No."

"I remember the way you used to, rolling, endlessly rolling thin little cigarettes, which you'd then smoke furiously in fast succession."

"Yes, I liked smoking. And, no, I don't smoke anymore, though most of the time I wish I did."

"I never understood," says Maggie, "this business of smoking: the attraction, the obsession, how it drives people. Junk I understand, after all, as you know, I've fucked a lot of junkies in my time. But I never smoked. So I don't get it, the awfulness of giving up, why it's so hard. Tell me, what's it like?"

So she begins to tell. Remembering, she warms to her topic, begins embroidering, dramatizing raw emotion. Then she sees the look on Maggie's face, a look she recalls: serious concentration masking pure acquisitive avidity.

She instantly shuts up. "But you write songs, you use your imagination. You must have some ideas."

"No," says Maggie. "None."

"None?"

"No, none." There's a long pause, then she adds, "Though I sometimes think about what Sartre said. You know."

"No, I don't know. Tell me, what did Sartre say?"

"Oh, you know, that every time he looked on a beautiful landscape, he wanted to smoke."

"Why?"

"Well, that's the mystery. I don't know, and neither did he."

"But you must have some ideas. And Sartre himself, didn't he hazard a guess?"

Maggie purses her lips; clearly she has some ideas and is loath to give them away. She frowns. At last she says, "I think he said that it was because he wanted to possess it, the landscape."

She has an inkling, at the time, that something is coming her way.

SHE FLIPPED through *Being and Nothingness*, scanned *The Emotions: Outline of a Theory*, but couldn't find any allusions to landscape and smoking. She asked some philosophers, but they were unhelpful; they said that smoking was a Sartrean red herring, not an issue central to philosophy. Her neighbor said he suspected that it was the landscape that was the red herring. Her hairdresser said, "Not at all, think of it this way: the cigarette can be possessed and smoked, and so, as you stand and contemplate the view, you have the illusion of possessing the landscape, too." This almost made sense at the time, but not quite; as a solution, its seduction was aphoristic, too enticingly neat—like the conservative view of smoking itself, which posits a model of conservation and equivalence, which says: when a cigarette is consumed, smoke is produced, what comes in goes out. Yes, but what takes place between the going and the coming, between the inside and outside, between figure and ground, object and landscape—what entangled conversions eventuate?

Her chances of coming up with answers to any of these questions were, she realized, pretty thin so long as she remained without precise philosophical reference, without cigarettes, without landscape. So she packed a bag and went to where there was landscape, to the Blue Mountains outside Sydney. In her rucksack she carried Sartre and a pack of Camels. She had no intention of opening either but hoped that they would perform like fetishes: when in alchemical relation with the landscape, they would act to magically produce a solution.

After a long hike through the Grose Valley and a steep climb up jagged rocky paths, she emerges out of the damp green underworld into sunlight, finding herself suddenly on a precipice, on the edge of the world. The landscape stretches forever, and it stretches her—like chewing gum—through space. She longs to be drawn from the edge, to plummet into the blue air and down into the darkness below. With equal intensity she longs to be grounded, to know where she stands: she wants a cigarette.

Is this what it means, she wonders, to be possessed? She understands now, in her body, that Sartre is right, that there is some connection between smoking and landscape and possession, and Maggie was right for intuiting this. She does not yet have the key to that connection, but she knows now that she will find it, and even if she never finds it, she has nevertheless been given a fetish that will, for good or ill, elicit writing.

Perhaps it's true, she thinks, that we are ready already possessed by words. They say, these days, that appropriation is just a making use of common knowledge, a kind of homage on occasion. But appropriation is not always an index of benign civility; it may also manifest as willfulness, a fierce variant of the will to knowledge. What is it that drives a person to seize hold of someone else's words, to wrest them away, to make them their own? And is it just a matter of words, just a matter of borrowing, putting into public circulation public property, letting loose ideas like smoke?

It is the fate of Sartre to be misquoted and misunderstood, perhaps, certainly misused, bartered, taken out of context. But a gem was tossed out that day in the doctor's waiting room when she was waiting for a gruesome prognosis, and she seized it. A little revenge, a tit for tat. Or perhaps it was, after all, an inadvertent gift.

SMOKING LANDSCAPE

Through the forest she runs, through damp green darkness, dodging creepers and swinging monkey ropes, tripping over moss-covered tree roots protruding into the path. Then suddenly she emerges onto a high plateau, mountains behind and around her.

Within minutes she is sitting on the edge of the escarpment. The light is beginning to fade, but slowly, it falls in bright shafts across the valley; the cliff face opposite is in shadow, the Mtrazi waters fall for half a mile, a silver streak against the blackness of the cliff wall.

Looking out over the Hondi Valley—in the Eastern Highlands of Zimbabwe—looking out into another country, into the wilds of Mozambique, she is revisited by an old sensation. For a moment it feels as though she has never left, as though nothing has changed, as though she has been sitting here on this rock for the last twenty-odd years. But then she remembers: everything has changed. Back then, she smoked without thinking; now—as the landscape pulls her from the edge, pulls her into the air, out and away—she thinks. And she wants. She remembers someone saying, "And every time he looked on a beautiful landscape he wanted to smoke," but she cannot remember who said it or when.

Back then, turning her back on Rhodesia, she had sat on the rock and worked her way through many cigarettes, blowing smoke out over the valley, watching it circle and snake and disappear, feeling that she herself was on the verge of disappearing. She knew that soon she would be gone, and even though she wanted never to return to this country so long as

it remained Rhodesia, even so she felt a sense of loss, the beginning of grief.

Even as she experienced this intimation of homesickness,
this brush with the sublime, all those years ago, she knew—
in some inchoate way—that the correlations between place
and self are always, like dodgy electrical connections, precarious. "Identity is not a sodding place, it's a relationship," her
grandfather used to mutter under his breath as they drove behind cars with huge bumper stickers saying "Proud to be
Rhodesian."

Now, even though she still experiences this landscape as
psychically and politically charged, she understands more
clearly that the power of place is phantasmatic. Rhodesia as a
country was a fiction (though people lived there), the border
between it and Mozambique was arbitrary (though crossing
the border could make a world of difference). As she sat there,
smoking, long ago, people were crossing into Mozambique
on foot, evading the official borders, there to train and participate in the intensifying guerrilla war. There are many
forms of exile, this she knew. Some people, more privileged,
go far away in airplanes, others go less far though more cir-
cuitously, on foot. Many of these people will never come
home. The survivors will return, but to another country—to
Zimbabwe.

IS IT JUST a matter of words, just a substitution of one name
for another, of Zimbabwe for Rhodesia? When in 1890 Cecil
Rhodes moved inland from the southern tip of Africa he invaded and appropriated several different kingdoms; boundaries were redrawn in flagrant disregard of indigenous relations to the land and a new country was created, named after
the imperial architect himself. Thus was set in place the be-
ginnings of settler legislation that would proceed through a
series of acts to partition the country into black and white
space (white farming lands and black reserves). Zimbabwe
was not the original name for the precolonial country—it was

the name of a beautiful ruined stone city in the heart of the country. Rhodes took this city as a sign of an earlier white civilization; the African nationalists in the 1960s took the name as a symbol of the continuity and strength of African culture.

EVEN THOUGH she now understands that the power of place is phantasmatic, nevertheless this landscape exerts a strange power; she feels that it will not let her go, that she is possessed by it and always will be. Or is it rather that she herself wants actively to possess: to possess this vista that speaks to her physically, that assures her of who she is?

"And every time he looked on a beautiful landscape he wanted to smoke." She remembers that the putative "he" is Sartre, but she has forgotten where she heard it, or what Sartre himself had to say on the matter.

Back then, she smoked without thinking. Now, she looks out on this landscape and wants to smoke, even though she has not touched a cigarette for ten years, and the thought of smoking scarcely ever skates across the surface of her mind. "Remember this," she tells herself, "the power of tobacco, too, is phantasmatic."

Looking down into the gorge she feels herself becoming light-headed, losing touch with the ground—stretched, like chewing gum, through space, she longs to be drawn over the edge, to plummet down into the darkness below. So she turns away from the view and fixes her gaze on the ground. Staring intently at the grass and stones, a fragment of color catches her eye. She leans down to look more closely: there nestled under the granite boulder on which she has been sitting is a slightly crumpled cigarette pack. A soft pack, white with a red star emblazoned on the front. You could hold it in the palm of your hand, even a child could close her hand around the pack, hear the cellophane rustle, smell the tobacco: strong, raw, a smell of heat as poles with cured leaves are pulled out from the furnaces.

Star cigarettes: cheap, enduring.

She uncrumples and prizes open the pack, holding her breath. Hoping. Inside is a half-smoked cigarette and a miniature bright green plastic lighter. As she looks at the pack in the palm of her hand, at the red star within the blue lasso, she hears a voice from the past:

> I didn't believe all the things my father used to tell me until I was in the bush myself. Then—well, you just had to believe. One time we had no tobacco, nothing to smoke. One of the boys went into a trance. He said that his father's brother had sent us some. His father's brother had died a long time before so we asked him how this would happen. He said that the tobacco would be brought to us by a snake. Then the boy came out of trance, went looking in the bush and found the snake. The body of the snake was all curled up but there in the middle was a lump of tobacco. The boy clapped to the snake very politely and the snake uncoiled itself. Then he took the tobacco and we all had a smoke.

She had once read these words—an account, given by a young man who had been a guerrilla, of help received from the ancestors during the liberation war—and now they come back to her, voiced; freed from the page the words rise up, prophetically, out of the landscape. Or call it the bush. She does not believe for a moment that her ancestors, parsimonious Presbyterians, have sent her this gift. But someone has, and so she whispers—to the trees and the mountains and the Mtarazi Falls: "Thank You." Then she takes out the half-squashed, half-smoked cigarette, holds it up against the sky and addresses it: "Now you are mine." She flicks the lighter. "But not for long."

"You are what you have." Words from somewhere else, some other past, some other book, rise up out of the bush. "You are what you have." She inhales and watches the tip of the cigarette flare, smolder, turn to ash.

But cigarettes aren't "things" like other things are things; you can't own a cigarette like you do a car, say. You can buy imitation Gaulthier dresses which become part of you, which signal your identity, but you can't "own" cigarettes in the same way, and neither, for that matter, can you possess a landscape, as though it were a mink coat. She tells herself this, but the cigarette—as it grows smaller and smaller— tells her something different.

Between her fingers, between her lips, it is a solid thing. But as soon as she begins smoking, so begins the destruction of its thingness. She absorbs the smoke into herself, and blows it out—watches it escape from her mouth, uncoil, and drift snakily over the landscape, to disperse and disappear into the valley below. She finds that the vertigo is subsiding. She can look down   can see villages, tiny but discernible, from which tendrils of smoke unfurl, rising up out of the valley. When she was last here there was nothing to be seen down there except dense foliage. A lot of trees have gone, she realizes, been cut down and used for firewood, and there are a lot more people living in the valley now. Things have changed. The landscape itself has changed.

Smoke from above and below intermingles, smoke rings lock in the air. For the first time she has an inkling of what people mean when they talk of tobacco as the sign of signs. It is not simply that it stands in place of something else. As a sign it *acts*. Smoking mediates one's relation to the world. It has quelled her vertigo for instance; in smoking the cigarette she smokes the landscape, takes it in, makes it her own. For Sartre, she imagines, the cigarette and by extension smoking epitomizes the will to possess. So to give up is a good thing: it means you relinquish this appropriative relation to the world.

A good thing is one thing. Actuality is something else altogether. No wonder he found it so hard, poor old Sartre— always thinking about giving up smoking, and giving up smoking, and taking up smoking again. All that time spent whining about tobacco! All that time he could have spent on philosophy! Of course, if smoking is a sign then it is not an essence, it takes its place in a network, among other signs, other ways of mediating one's relation to the world; but if the cigarette is the perfect sign, then in actuality, there is no substitute—or nothing else that quite does the trick.

She has smoked her way to the end of the cigarette. The light is fading fast, she can hear the Mtarazi Falls but cannot see the ribbon of water—across the gorge there is only blackness. She smoothes out the empty pack, feels—rather than sees—the red star, and the blue lasso caught in midair, and pockets it carefully. The cigarette is gone but the miniature lighter remains. She flicks it and a tiny flame springs up. A lighter is no substitute for a cigarette, but who knows where it might take you?

LIFE-GIVING MIST

∞

It is said that the smoke of tobacco was called "life-giving mist" by the Mbuyá-guarani of South America because they believed it to be the source of vitality, an attribute of the god of spring, the patron of shamans.

Tobacco smoking here is associated with the sacred, with ritual, with consciousness changing. Smoke is a medium between the natural and supernatural worlds, between mortals and gods; and so it is an activity set apart from the everyday and from ordinary people. Only shamans may smoke.

And the shamans smoke a lot, for the gods are greedy and the gods need nicotine. Smoke is their food, and, with the craving of an addict, they await gifts of sustenance from their chief provider—human beings. In the Mundurucú tobacco myth, even the Mother of Tobacco—who created tobacco smoke sui generis and carried it in a calabash from which she periodically sucked her vital sustenance—died as soon as she ran out of the life-giving smoke. On the whole, though, a supply is guaranteed and an equilibrium sustained.

The Native Americans codified addiction by attributing to the gods a craving and a dependency, but the relation between gods and mortals, it seems to me, is not codified in terms of abject dependence, but rather in terms of an economy of exchange that revolves around reciprocity and interdependence. The gods require tobacco smoke from mortals, and in turn the mortals have access to the spirit world through tobacco. On the one hand, tobacco transports mortals into the realm of the spirits, where they can learn how "to see" things that are beyond the physical field of vision. They can participate in a life of bliss, devoid of the suffering, starvation, and death of their own world. On the other hand, the spirits and their sphere are attracted through tobacco to the physical earth, where some of the transcendent blessings of their metaphysical world are conferred upon humans.

Nowadays the everyday smoking of tobacco for pleasure is widespread among the Indians of North and South America, but in some places a distinction is often still made between indigenous and white man's tobacco. Native tobacco was and sometimes still is associated with real intoxication, to the point of a radical altering of consciousness or psychedelic trance. And often an entire and complex metaphysical universe is literally held together and sustained by tobacco smoke.

Writing about the uses of divine tobacco and regretting the passing of this way of life, an anthropologist/historian notes:

> There is deep beauty there which we, in our materialistic world, bombarded with advertising on television and in print of some young man lighting a girl's cigarette as a prelude to conquest, are unable to share or even to perceive. The relationship is that of compline to a blast of the Beatles and their sad imitators.

I wonder. Magic always cuts both ways, and I for one wouldn't like to be at the mercy of a dark shaman. "Light" shamans blow tobacco smoke over patients and others in life-crisis situations, over objects, foodstuffs, the river and forest. Generally the purpose of this is purification, the reinvigoration of the weak and the warding off of evil spirits. "Dark" shamans, on the other hand, blow tobacco smoke in order to debilitate and kill.

> *It is smoke that makes the shaman's breath visible and with it the benevolent or malevolent charges.*

The curious thing about tobacco is that it is both an upper and a downer, a depressant and a stimulant; it purifies and it kills. This curious fact is also what makes of tobacco a wondrous gift. It comes like manna from heaven when you're feeling low, that kind of Bressonian cornflakes-soaked-in-brandy low, a low that is soggy with sentiment but at the same time raked by agitation. A cigarette offers itself, you inhale, and the smoke insinuates your system, spreading instantaneous calm. You exhale, and the smoke, a life-giving mist, disperses blackness, cleansing the world—and your being—of grease and grime. Or perhaps you're lethargic, sitting at the computer like a crocodile awaiting its prey, and the screen is filled with emptiness, a stagnant muddy river. Suddenly a cigarette materializes and with it energy, a miraculous sharpening of the mind and teeth. Witness the arrival, on the river's edge, of an innocent backpacker. You open your mouth, blow smoke on the screen, clamp your jaws shut, and swallow whole your victim. Then spit it out—bloodied limbs and lacerated words hurtle onto the screen, making up a lurid story. Or perhaps you're in a sweat, wanting her and wanting courage, desire seeping out of every pore, but you can't bring yourself to make that move, to reach out, to say: Let's do it. Masquerading nonchalance, you offer a cigarette and she takes it, and suddenly you don't even need to say it, you're moving away together.

These qualities, it sometimes seems, are intrinsic to tobacco, the property of every cigarette. And yet this property is merely virtual; anticipation, we might say, produces the magical realism of quotidian immanence. The merely virtual possesses a power to be reckoned with. We project, we invest the object with all our desires, all our needs for curative affect, all our fantasies of divine transcendence, all our fears of dirt and contamination and death. And it—not the object in itself but that smoky ring of desire in which the object is conjured into being and circulates—returns us to ourselves more complete, almost completely satisfied.

For the smoker, smoking becomes second nature—like breathing and talking and eating and touching. There was a

time when it would almost go unnoticed. Certainly in our society, smoking as a practice is part of quotidian existence: it
isn't ritualized, mediated by and confined to the realm of the
shamans. Nevertheless, every act of smoking is potentially
ceremonial, a staged performance of the everyday, a way of
enabling so many daily pleasures and struggles, repetitious
moments of work and leisure. Take the first cigarette after
quitting, the lapsing cigarette, the breaking of the fast, the
sundering of continuity. This cigarette is unlike any other,
and yet the smoking of it enacts a commemoration of other
acts and is thus a ritualized reenactment: it is like a substitution of the first time, a reentry into the continuity of life, relationships, a social fabric that holds together. It banishes absence, death, denial, starvation.

No longer does smoking go unnoticed. Now "smoking"
rhymes with "giving up" and the mediate term is "dirty." In
every crook and cranny, in every private space as well as public, there are spies and sniffer dogs and circus ringmasters
whipping up a frenzy of abstinence. The nonsmoking campaign operates within an economy of moralism, within a
rhetoric of abhorrence that appeals to "the common good."
The campaign relies on an incantatory invocation of "dirt,"
and terms like *filth* and *disgusting* and *contamination* are conjured into being, breathed out by the great dragon-machine
of puritan capitalism, breathed over us grimy sinners like a
malevolent breath. And like vampires engulfed by the right-
eous purity of garlic fumes, we wither (or so mythology sup-
poses). Designated leperlike smokers are made to feel socially
guilty, as though acting criminally against the common good.
Of course smoking is no more "dirty" than gas fumes, the
sewerage pumped into our bays, industrial effluents. It might
sometimes be lethal, but it's not this notion that's deployed as
a weapon so much as the idea of "contamination."

Of course you don't acquire addiction of any sort through
contamination, through kissing or being in the same room,
say. But popular mythology has always shrouded drugs in this

mystical aura. And there's guilt, or punishment, by association: you can be polluted, hooked, and doomed involuntarily—through passive smoking. A discourse conceived in terms of passivity and negativity sets in place a scenario of abjection and guilt and "giving up" particular to smoking. You don't often "give up" heroin, say—you stop using, kick the habit, go cold turkey. The metaphors are more violent.

Of course you don't acquire addiction of any sort through contamination, through kissing, for instance, or being in the same room. You don't catch it physically, that is; it's not registered, deposited in your body as an itemized germ or on your skin as a greasy stain. But kissing or even being in the same room may, of course, have dangerous consequences. There is a forgetfulness to passion and a tenacity to sensate memory, and smoke can weave a spell of empathy where least expected. In life-crisis situations, or even in the midst of celebration or unexpected intimacy, you might reach for a cigarette, and blow smoke out, smoke like life-giving mist that purifies and reinvigorates the weak and wards off evil spirits.

IN TRANSIT

If the smoke from the tip of my cigarette and the ink from the nib of my pen flowed with equal ease, I should be in the Arcadia of my writing. WALTER BENJAMIN, *One-Way Street*

VIETATO FUMARE! At the Rome airport there are signs everywhere, forbidding smoking, and everywhere the signs are ignored.

As she enters the departure terminal, she sees a man about to step onto the escalator. He lights up a cigarette, he lights up like a man who's been in an office all day, an office where you aren't allowed to smoke. He lights up with great deliberation and pleasure, as though he's been anticipating this moment all day. And then he exhales, slowly, a huge plume of smoke. As he ascends, as the escalator glides upward, so the plume of smoke rises with him.

Watching this scene, she finds herself imagining it in words. She begins, for the first time, to imagine writing. To imagine writing, rather than to imagine smoking.

NOTES

A FISHY SMELL

Lévi-Strauss assigns tobacco Claude Lévi-Strauss, *From Honey to Ashes*, trans. John and Doreen Weightman (Chicago: University of Chicago Press, 1973), pp. 17–18.

"tobacco symbolizes the symbolic," says Derrida Jacques Derrida, *Given Time: 1, Counterfeit Money*, trans. Peggy Kamuf (Chicago: University of Chicago Press, 1992), p. 112.

BURIAL

not quite the same Paul Willemen, writing about the film *Pursued*, refers to psychoanalytic theorist Serge Leclaire's reflections on the pleasure of smoking cigars. Willemen comments that in this instance it would be possible to substitute film for tobacco: "he maintains that it is not the special taste or aroma which produce pleasure, but 'that slight giddiness which springs from the *not quite the same* in which we recognize *the same* tobacco.'" See Paul Willemen, "The Fugitive Subject," in *Raoul Walsh*, ed. Phil Hardy (Edinburgh: Edinburgh Film Festival, 1974), p. 65.

But a petty thought, as Zarathustra says Friedrich Nietzsche, "Thus Spoke Zarathustra," in *The Portable Nietzsche*, ed. and trans. Walter Kaufmann (New York: Penguin, 1982), p. 201.

YAKANDANDA

the Aborigines, who traveled across the Australian continent with smoldering fire-sticks This account of Aboriginal fire practices is derived from Stephen J. Pyne, *Burning Bush: A Fire History of Australia* (Sydney: Allen and Unwin, 1992).

In the beginning there is the burning of the tobacco beds   This
　　account of tobacco curing is based on Frank Clements and
　　Edward Harben, *Leaf of Gold: The Story of Rhodesian Tobacco*
　　(London: Methuen, 1962).

THE BODY HAS A MIND OF ITS OWN

George Orwell's anecdote   "Keep the Aspidistra Flying," in *George
　　Orwell* (New York: Octopus/Heinemann, 1980), p. 615.
Mr. Leopold Bloom   James Joyce, *Ulysses* (London: John Lane, the
　　Bodley Head, 1967), p. 65.
*Sinking like the dormouse into a comforting bed of delphiniums blue
　　and geraniums red*   In the A. A. Milne poem "The Dormouse
　　and the Doctor," the doctor mistakenly concludes that the
　　dormouse is ill because he stays in bed—a bed "Of delphini-
　　ums (blue) and geraniums (red)." The doctor replants the bed
　　with "endless chrysanthemums (yellow and white)," which
　　really do make the dormouse ill. The dormouse finds a solu-
　　tion, however: he lies on his front with his paws to his eyes,
　　imagining he is in a bed of "delphiniums (blue) and geraniums
　　(red)." See A. A. Milne, *When We Were Very Young* (London:
　　Methuen, 1925), pp. 66–70.

WHITE MAN

"The Hollanders gradually advance into the country . . ."   Berthold
　　Laufer, Wilfrid D. Hambly, and Ralph Linton, *Tobacco and Its
　　Use in Africa*, Anthropology leaflet 29 (Chicago: Field
　　Museum of Natural History, 1930), p. 10.
"To illustrate the rapidity and extraordinary profits . . ."   Major
　　Arthur Glyn Leonard, *How We Made Rhodesia* (1896; reprint,
　　Bulawayo: Books of Rhodesia, 1973), p. 35.
In the teens one of the most popular Rhodesian cigarettes   Clements
　　and Harben, *Leaf of Gold*, p. 62.
In France in the seventeenth century   Laufer et al., *Tobacco and Its
　　Use in Africa*, p. 2.
Jim Jarmusch has said   Jonathan Rosenbaum, "A Gun Up Your
　　Ass: An Interview with Jim Jarmusch," *Cineaste* 22 (1996): 21.

The Savage Hits Back   Julius E. Lips, trans. Vincent Benson
(New York: University Books, 1966) p. 199, fig. 176.

TRANSLATION (A GIFT OF OPIUM)

One of the most lucid drawings   Jean Cocteau, *Opium: Journal d'une
désintoxication* (Paris: Stock, 1976), p. 17.

SEASICKNESS

She is seasick—on dry land   This notion of "seasickness on dry
land" is taken from Franz Kafka. See Walter Benjamin, "Franz   229
Kafka," in *Illuminations*, ed. Hannah Arendt, trans. Harry
Zohn (London: Fontana, 1973), p. 130.

"A psychoanalyst sits in his office . . ."   Géza Róheim, *Children of the
Desert: The Western Tribes of Central Australia*, vol. 1 (New
York: Harper and Row, 1976), p. xvii.

TO BUBBLE AND RUMBLE (LIKE AN ELEPHANT)

*Even today it is women, and only women, who smoke an elaborate
calabash pipe*   See D. K. Parkinson, "The Batonga Pipe,"
NADA (Native Affairs Department Annual) 10, no. 1 (1969):
74–75; H. Ellert, *The Material Culture of Zimbabwe* (Harare:
Longman Zimbabwe, 1984), pp. 123–26; A. K. H. Weinrich
(Sister Mary Aquinas), *The Tonga People on the Southern Shore of
Lake Kariba* (Gwelo: Mambo Press, 1977).

*Smokers in action . . . can be heard . . . making a loud noise very much
like the rumbling of elephants*   John L. Salmon, "Among the
Wild Batonka Tribe of Southern Rhodesia," ten-page unpub-
lished essay, National Archives of Zimbabwe, p. 5.

David Livingstone   David and Charles Livingstone, *Narrative of
an Expedition to the Zambesi and Its Tributaries; and of the
Discovery of the Lakes Shirwa and Nyassa, 1858–1864* (New
York: Harper and Brothers, 1866), pp. 256–57.

BOMBS OR BUMS (METAPHOR)

Wag the Dog *situation*   The movie *Wag the Dog* (dir. Barry
Levinson, United States, 1997) is a black comedy about an

attempt by a Washington spin doctor and a Hollywood pro-
ducer to deflect a presidential sex scandal by fabricating a
media war (in Albania).

TRACED BY (A SLIGHT SENSE OF) BITTERNESS
It is an old black-and-white photograph   Reproduced in *Zimbabwe
    ˙Epic*, a pictorial sourcebook assembled from the holdings of
    the National Archives, researched and compiled by P. C.
    Mazikana and I. J. Johnstone, edited and designed by R. G. S.
    Douglas (1982; reprint, Harare: National Archives, 1984), p.
    118.
Following the word nyoka, *I discover*   The historical information in
    this story is derived from Barry Kosmin, "The Inyoka
    Tobacco Industry of the Shangwe People: The Displacement
    of a Pre-Colonial Economy in Southern Rhodesia,
    1898–1938," in *The Roots of Rural Poverty in Central and
    Southern Africa*, ed. Robin Palmer and Neil Parsons (London:
    Heinemann Educational, 1977), pp. 268–88.
*"In Rhodesia we have all the factors making for the building up of a
    great industry. . . ."*   "Development of the Rhodesia Tobacco
    Industry," *The African World* 44 (6 September 1913): 246.

TO REMEMBER (TO FIND YOURSELF IN FRAGMENTS)
He's Gregory Peck   In *Mirage*, dir. Edward Dmytryk, United
    States, 1965.

TO FORGET
"We photograph things in order to drive them out of our minds."
    Cited by Roland Barthes, *Camera Lucida: Reflections on
    Photography* (New York: Hill and Wang, 1981), p. 53.

CHAOS
Yet if every passion, as Benjamin remarks   Benjamin, *Illuminations*,
    p. 60.

STRANGE ATTRACTORS

Falconetti   Renée Falconetti, star of the film *La Passion de Jeanne d'Arc*, dir. Carl Theodor Dreyer, France, 1927.

Lucy . . . gets a job . . . advertising cough syrup   "Lucy Does a Commercial," episode 30 of *I Love Lucy*, first screened 5 May 1952.

A LYCANTHROPIC AGE (THE WRITING CURE)

Harold Holt   A former Australian prime minister who disappeared from a beach in 1967. His body was never found, but he was generally presumed drowned.

A BOIL ABOUT TO BURST

she . . . imagined she was H. D.   H. D. is the nom de plume of the poet Hilda Doolittle, who wrote a book about her analysis with Freud (*Tribute to Freud* [New York: Pantheon, 1956]).

MOUTHING

The person from whom I heard this story   Stephen Greenblatt, in a lecture that subsequently found its way into *Marvelous Possessions: The Wonder of the New World* (Chicago: University of Chicago Press, 1991), pp. 57, 63.

APPETITE

"Whence the narrow constipation of a strictly human attitude . . ."   Georges Batailles, "Mouth," in *Visions of Excess: Selected Writings, 1927–1939*, ed. and intro. Allan Stoekl, trans. Allan Stoekl with Carl R. Lovitt and Donald M. Leslie Jr. (Minneapolis: University of Minnesota Press, 1985), p. 60.

"Men and women and children would gather about me . . ."   Laufer et al., *Tobacco and Its Use in Africa*, p. 21.

But there are other cultures, such as the Melanesian   See Marilyn Strathern, *The Gender of the Gift: Problems with Women and Problems with Society in Melanesia* (Berkeley: University of

California Press, 1988), especially pp. 144–45, 288–98.

Nervous Conditions Tsitsi Dangarembga, *Nervous Conditions* (Seattle: Seal Press, 1989). See also Anthony Chennells, "Authorizing Women, Women's Authoring: Tsitsi Dangarembga's *Nervous Conditions*," in *New Writing from Southern Africa: Authors Who Have Become Prominent since 1980*, ed. Emmanuel Ngara (London: James Currey, 1996), pp. 59–75.

Freud shows how the antagonism of projection and introjection See J. Laplanche and J. B. Pontalis, *The Language of Psycho-analysis*, trans. Donald Nicholson-Smith (London: Hogarth Press, 1973), p. 230.

"My case is not unique . . ." Violette Leduc, *La Bâtarde*, trans. Derek Coltman (New York: Farrar, Straus and Giroux, 1965), p. 3.

"I have resolved on an enterprise which has no precedent . . ." Jean-Jacques Rousseau, *The Confessions of Jean-Jacques Rousseau*, trans. J. M. Cohen (1781; reprint, Harmondsworth, Eng., 1953, p. 17).

LIONS DON'T SMOKE

"The public is tired of savages. . . ." See *Nonfiction Films From the Teens*, ed. Daan De Klerk and Nico Hertogs (Amsterdam: Stichting Nederlands Filmmuseum, 1994), p. 62.

FOG DRINKING

Schivelbusch tells us Wolfgang Schivelbusch, *Tastes of Paradise: A Social History of Spices, Stimulants, and Intoxicants*, trans. David Jacobson (New York: Vintage, 1992), p. 96.

"Australian wool, Brazilian coffee, Cuban sugar . . ." "The Tourist in 'Tobaccoland,'" *Africa Calls* 14 (July–August 1962): 20.

"Finally, as there is no likelihood . . ." "Development of the Rhodesia Tobacco Industry," p. 246.

But of course Byron's breezy words Written on the wind perhaps, but blown hither and thither fortuitously, resonating more recently in the marvelous manifestation of Richard Klein's *Cigarettes Are Sublime* (London: Picador, 1995). Quoting the poem from which these lines are drawn, Klein comments: "To Byron . . . belongs the credit for having been the first to understand the aesthetic pleasure of tobacco in connection with the eighteenth-century doctrines of the sublime, in a poem entitled 'Sublime Tobacco'" (p. 198, note 2).

KETTLE LOGIC (THE ART OF SEPARATION)

kettle logic This notion comes from Freud. Although he does not actually use the term "kettle logic" he does tell a story about a borrowed kettle in order to illustrate a certain kind of sophistry. See Sigmund Freud, *Jokes and Their Relation to the Unconscious*, standard ed., vol. 8, pp. 62 and 205.

I DONE A LOTTA BAD THINGS

"an anterior state of suicide . . ." Antonin Artaud, *Artaud Anthology*, ed. Jack Hirschman (San Francisco: City Lights Books, 1965), p. 60.

THE SMOKING ROOM

Think of the mural Men without Women This mural was acquired by the Metropolitan Museum of Art in 1974 and renamed simply *Mural*. Georgia O'Keeffe was hired to paint the mural for the Ladies' Powder Room, but it was never completed. See Peter Wollen, *Raiding the Ice Box: Reflections on Twentieth-Century Culture* (London: Verso, 1993), p. 61; and Lowery Stokes Sims, *Stuart Davis, American Painter* (New York: Metropolitan Museum of Art, 1991).

"Whatever Aristotle and all of philosophy might say . . ." Cited by Jacques Derrida, *Given Time*, pp. 112–13.

Michel Serres identifies Don Juan Michel Serres, *Literature, Science, Philosophy* (Baltimore: Johns Hopkins University Press, 1982), pp. 3 and 13.

Derrida notes *Given Time*, p. 115.

Lola Montez caught this habit from George Sand For a captivating photograph of Montez with cigarette, see Schivelbusch, *Tastes of Paradise*, p. 124.

Prisoner   This classic serial melodrama about women in prison aired from 1979 to 1986 on Network Ten in Australia, and in other countries as *Cell Block H.*

KINDNESS (OR, THE WEREWOLF COMES HOME)
Brecht's account of the Temptation to be Good   This is a leitmotiv that recurs throughout Brecht's work. As the singer puts it bluntly to Grusha in *The Caucasian Chalk Circle*: "Fearful is the seductive power of goodness!" (Bertolt Brecht, *The Caucasian Chalk Circle*, in *Two Plays by Bertolt Brecht*, trans. Eric Bentley [New York: New American Library, 1983], p. 147).

THOSE PLACES IN THE BODY THAT HAVE NO LANGUAGE EITHER
He read to her from a book   Michel de Certeau's *The Practice of Everyday Life*, trans. Steven Rendall (Berkeley: University of California Press, 1985), p. 162.
A very American painting   Love of Winter by George Wesley Bellows, 1914 (in the collection of the Art Institute of Chicago).

HABIT
The Woman Who Worries about Everything   In Nicole Hollander's *Female Problems: An Unhelpful Guide* (New York: Dell, 1995), p. 24.

A SLEEPING PROBLEM
"That'll be the day"   John Wayne, as Ethan Edwards in *The Searchers*, uses this phrase repeatedly.
"To be happy is to be able to become aware of oneself without fright." Walter Benjamin, *One-Way Street and Other Writings*, trans. Edmund Jephcott and Shorter Kingsley (London: NLB, 1979), p. 71.
"And I am desolate and sick of an old passion"   Ernest Dowson, "Non Sum Qualis Eram Bonae Sub Regno Cynarae," in *The Poems of Ernest Dowson* (London: John Lane, the Bodley Head, 1922), pp. 27–28. This line recurs as a chorus throughout the

poem, which ends thus: "And I am desolate and sick of an old passion, / Yea, hungry for the lips of my desire: / I have been faithful to thee, Cynara! In my fashion."

LIGHTING UP

Canetti tells a tale of an arsonist   Elias Canetti, *Crowds and Power*, trans. Carol Stewart (New York: Viking Press, 1966), p. 93.

POSSESSED

Charmaine Solomon   The Complete Asian Cookbook (Sydney: Lansdowne Press, 1979).

SMOKING LANDSCAPE

"I didn't believe all the things my father used to tell me . . ." Quoted in David Lan, *Guns and Rain: Guerrillas and Spirit Mediums in Zimbabwe* (London and Berkeley: James Currey and University of California Press, 1985), p. xv.

"You are what you have."   Allusions in this story to the relation between Sartre and cigarettes are indebted to Richard Kline's discussion in chap. 1 of *Cigarettes Are Sublime*, especially pp. 28–40.

LIFE-GIVING MIST

It is said that the smoke of tobacco   Much in this story is derived from Johannes Wilbert, "Magico-Religious Use of Tobacco among South American Indians," in *Spirits, Shamans, and Stars: Perspectives from South America*, ed. David L. Browman and Ronald A. Schwarz (Paris: Mouton, 1979), pp. 13–38.

"There is deep beauty . . ."   J. Eric S. Thompson, *Maya History and Religion* (Norman: University of Oklahoma Press, 1970), pp. 122–23.

GLOSSARY

amacimbi: dried caterpillar

biltong: dried meat

barbies: barbecues

bowser: a gas pump

bundu: bush

dagga: marijuana

duco: a type of paint often used on the bodywork of a motor vehicle

dunny: an outside toilet

fibro: compressed asbestos and cement used for building materials; also used to describe structures made of such materials

"Humba!": "Go Away!"

ikhiwa: white person

kopje: rocky hill

laminex: a high-pressure laminated plastic surfacing material, as for tables, kitchen counters, etc.

mazamban: ground nuts

mbanje: marijuana

mealies: maize

moggy: slang for *cat*

mombies: cattle

N'anga: spirit medium

Ndebele: one of the two main indigenous languages spoken in Zimbabwe, the other being *Shona*. Ndebele is spoken by the Ndebele people who live in Matabeleland

petrol: gasoline

pram: shortened form of *perambulator,* a four-wheeled baby carriage

Shona: the language spoken by the Shona people who inhabit Mashonaland

tsotsis: ruffians, gangsters

turn-up for the books: colloquial expression meaning a surprise or an unexpected reversal of fortune

vlei: low-lying marshy land